W9-BFE-636

OPPOSING
VIEWPOINTS®
SERIES

Police Brutality

Other Books of Related Interest:

Opposing Viewpoints Series

American Values

Community Policing

Corporate Social Responsibility

Gun Violence

World Peace

At Issue Series

Domestic Surveillance

Guns and Crime

Is Society Becoming Less Civil?

Minorities and the Law

Self-Defense Laws

Current Controversies Series

Bullying

Death Penalty

Racial Profiling

Violence in the Media

"Congress shall make no law . . . abridging the freedom of speech, or of the press."

First Amendment to the US Constitution

The basic foundation of our democracy is the First Amendment guarantee of freedom of expression. The Opposing Viewpoints series is dedicated to the concept of this basic freedom and the idea that it is more important to practice it than to enshrine it.

OPPOSING
VIEWPOINTS®
SERIES

Police Brutality

Michael Ruth, Book Editor

GREENHAVEN PRESS
A part of Gale, Cengage Learning

GALE
CENGAGE Learning·

Farmington Hills, Mich • San Francisco • New York • Waterville, Maine
Meriden, Conn • Mason, Ohio • Chicago

GALE
CENGAGE Learning

Judy Galens, *Manager, Frontlist Acquisitions*

© 2016 Greenhaven Press, a part of Gale, Cengage Learning.

Gale and Greenhaven Press are registered trademarks used herein under license.

For more information, contact:
Greenhaven Press
27500 Drake Rd.
Farmington Hills, MI 48331-3535
Or you can visit our Internet site at gale.cengage.com

For product information and technology assistance, contact us at

Gale Customer Support, 1-800-877-4253
For permission to use material from this text or product, submit all requests online at
www.cengage.com/permissions

Further permissions questions can be emailed to permissionrequest@cengage.com

Articles in Greenhaven Press anthologies are often edited for length to meet page requirements. In addition, original titles of these works are changed to clearly present the main thesis and to explicitly indicate the author's opinion. Every effort is made to ensure that Greenhaven Press accurately reflects the original intent of the authors. Every effort has been made to trace the owners of copyrighted material.

Cover Image Ilya Andriyanov/Shutterstock.com

LIBRARY OF CONGRESS CATALOGING-IN-PUBLICATION DATA

Police brutality (Greenhaven Press)
  Police brutality / Michael Ruth, book editor.
    pages cm. -- (Opposing viewpoints)
  Includes bibliographical references and index.
  ISBN 978-0-7377-7518-1 (hardcover) -- ISBN 978-0-7377-7519-8 (pbk.)
  1. Police brutality--United States. 2. Discrimination in law enforcement--United
  States. 3. Police--Complaints against--United States. 4. Police-community
  relations--United States. I. Ruth, Michael (Book editor) II. Title.
  HV8141.P57 2016
  363.2'32--dc23
                              2015028070

Printed in Mexico
1 2 3 4 5 6 7 20 19 18 17 16

Contents

Why Consider Opposing Viewpoints?   11

Introduction   14

Chapter 1: Are Police Using Excessive Force?

Chapter Preface   19

1. Police Brutality Must Be Stopped   21
   Richard Rowe

2. There Is Conflicting Information   30
   on Police Brutality
   John Wihbey

3. Police Are Racist Against Minorities   39
   Linn Washington Jr.

4. Police Are Not Racist Against Minorities   46
   James B. Comey

5. Police Militarization Is a Problem in America   55
   Carolyn Davis

6. Public Safety Requires Police Militarization   61
   Jazz Shaw

Periodical and Internet Sources Bibliography   67

Chapter 2: Is Police Brutality a Widespread Problem in the United States?

Chapter Preface   69

1. Seven Reasons Police Brutality Is Systemic,   71
   Not Anecdotal
   Bonnie Kristian

2. History Indicates Varied Results in Improving   77
Police Brutality in America
Nicole Flatow

3. Police Brutality Is a Growing American Epidemic   87
Colin Ochs

4. Police Brutality Is Not a Growing Epidemic   93
Jack Kerwick

5. White America's Silence on Police Brutality   98
Is Consent
Donovan X. Ramsey

6. Police Brutality in America Is About Class,   104
Not Race
Joseph Kishore

Periodical and Internet Sources Bibliography   111

Chapter 3: How Can Police Brutality Be Stopped?

Chapter Preface   113

1. Body Cameras Will Stop Police Brutality   115
Adam Schiff

2. Body Cameras Will Not Stop Police Brutality   120
Shahid Buttar

3. Body Cameras Are Helpful but Insufficient   127
for Stopping Police Brutality
Matthew Kovac

4. Americans Must Continue Protesting   133
Police Brutality
Juan Thompson

5. Americans Should Value, Not Protest, the Police   137
Charlie Dent

6. Civilian Oversight of Police Could Stop Brutality   142
Michael S. Rozeff

7. Civilian Oversight of Police Has Benefits   148
and Disadvantages
Pete Eyre

Periodical and Internet Sources Bibliography   157

Chapter 4: What Is the US Government's Response to Police Brutality?

Chapter Preface   159

1. The Federal Government Is Failing to Correct   161
Police Brutality
Barry Sussman

2. The Federal Government Is Enthusiastically   168
Combating Police Brutality
Jessica Wehrman and Jack Torry

3. Obama Is Correct to Separate Police Brutality   173
from Racism
Paul Joseph Watson

4. Obama Is Wrong to Separate Police Brutality   178
from Racism
Keeanga-Yamahtta Taylor

5. The Department of Justice Cannot Correct   187
All Police Brutality
Imani Gandy

6. The Department of Justice Can Help   193
Correct Police Brutality
Sarah Childress

Periodical and Internet Sources Bibliography   202

For Further Discussion   203

Organizations to Contact   206

Bibliography of Books   211

Index   215

Why Consider Opposing Viewpoints?

> *"The only way in which a human being can make some approach to knowing the whole of a subject is by hearing what can be said about it by persons of every variety of opinion and studying all modes in which it can be looked at by every character of mind. No wise man ever acquired his wisdom in any mode but this."*
>
> John Stuart Mill

In our media-intensive culture it is not difficult to find differing opinions. Thousands of newspapers and magazines and dozens of radio and television talk shows resound with differing points of view. The difficulty lies in deciding which opinion to agree with and which "experts" seem the most credible. The more inundated we become with differing opinions and claims, the more essential it is to hone critical reading and thinking skills to evaluate these ideas. Opposing Viewpoints books address this problem directly by presenting stimulating debates that can be used to enhance and teach these skills. The varied opinions contained in each book examine many different aspects of a single issue. While examining these conveniently edited opposing views, readers can develop critical thinking skills such as the ability to compare and contrast authors' credibility, facts, argumentation styles, use of persuasive techniques, and other stylistic tools. In short, the Opposing Viewpoints Series is an ideal way to attain the higher-level thinking and reading skills so essential in a culture of diverse and contradictory opinions.

In addition to providing a tool for critical thinking, Opposing Viewpoints books challenge readers to question their own strongly held opinions and assumptions. Most people form their opinions on the basis of upbringing, peer pressure, and personal, cultural, or professional bias. By reading carefully balanced opposing views, readers must directly confront new ideas as well as the opinions of those with whom they disagree. This is not to argue simplistically that everyone who reads opposing views will—or should—change his or her opinion. Instead, the series enhances readers' understanding of their own views by encouraging confrontation with opposing ideas. Careful examination of others' views can lead to the readers' understanding of the logical inconsistencies in their own opinions, perspective on why they hold an opinion, and the consideration of the possibility that their opinion requires further evaluation.

Evaluating Other Opinions

To ensure that this type of examination occurs, Opposing Viewpoints books present all types of opinions. Prominent spokespeople on different sides of each issue as well as well-known professionals from many disciplines challenge the reader. An additional goal of the series is to provide a forum for other, less known, or even unpopular viewpoints. The opinion of an ordinary person who has had to make the decision to cut off life support from a terminally ill relative, for example, may be just as valuable and provide just as much insight as a medical ethicist's professional opinion. The editors have two additional purposes in including these less known views. One, the editors encourage readers to respect others' opinions—even when not enhanced by professional credibility. It is only by reading or listening to and objectively evaluating others' ideas that one can determine whether they are worthy of consideration. Two, the inclusion of such viewpoints encourages the important critical thinking skill of objectively evaluating an author's credentials and bias. This evaluation will illuminate an author's reasons for taking a particular stance on an issue and will aid in readers' evaluation of the author's ideas.

It is our hope that these books will give readers a deeper understanding of the issues debated and an appreciation of the complexity of even seemingly simple issues when good and honest people disagree. This awareness is particularly important in a democratic society such as ours in which people enter into public debate to determine the common good. Those with whom one disagrees should not be regarded as enemies but rather as people whose views deserve careful examination and may shed light on one's own.

Thomas Jefferson once said that "difference of opinion leads to inquiry, and inquiry to truth." Jefferson, a broadly educated man, argued that "if a nation expects to be ignorant and free ... it expects what never was and never will be." As individuals and as a nation, it is imperative that we consider the opinions of others and examine them with skill and discernment. The Opposing Viewpoints series is intended to help readers achieve this goal.

David L. Bender and Bruno Leone,
Founders

Introduction

American outrage over police brutality has appeared in bursts throughout modern times. It flared during the racially charged era of the 1960s and 1970s, when the relationship between African Americans and the police became especially tumultuous. In 1965, for example, Alabama state police carried out violent acts against African Americans who were marching peacefully from Selma to Montgomery to advocate civil rights. In 1985, eighteen-year-old Mark Davidson was arrested by police in New York for selling a small amount of marijuana. He was then taken to a police station, where officers beat him and tortured him with a stun gun. The police beating of motorist Rodney King in Los Angeles in 1991, and the subsequent acquittal of the officers involved, sparked the 1992 Los Angeles riots, which caused widespread city destruction and more than fifty deaths.

The King incident, however, was significantly different from previous such cases in that it marked one of the first times that an occurrence of police brutality had been recorded on video. The evidence did not help in charging King's assailants with crimes (though several of the officers were later successfully prosecuted in federal court), but it fundamentally changed the American public's perception of police officers as incorruptible forces of virtue. As the 1990s came to a close and the twenty-first century began, reports of police misconduct against citizens began appearing in the news more frequently, mostly due to the advancement and widespread availability of recording technology such as smartphones. In the mid-2010s, the importance of this technology in protecting the civil rights of American citizens from police aggression became a serious topic of discussion. In 2014 and 2015, numerous incidents of police brutality were recorded on video and released to the public, with varying results.

A prominent example occurred in July 2014 in Staten Island, New York, where police attempted to arrest forty-three-year-old Eric Garner for selling untaxed cigarettes. As Garner protested the charge and the confrontation escalated, Garner's friend Ramsey Orta began recording the exchange between Garner and the police with his cell phone. The video, later released to the media, showed Officer Daniel Pantaleo placing Garner in what appeared to be a choke hold, which ultimately caused Garner's death by compressing his airway. Despite visual evidence of the event, however, a grand jury in December 2014 elected not to indict Pantaleo.

Orta, meanwhile, claimed in the press that his video documentation of Garner's death had made him a target of New York police who wanted to exact vengeance on him. In February 2015, Orta was sentenced to two months in New York's Rikers Island prison complex for drug crimes. He soon stopped eating after hearing reports that numerous other prisoners had found rat poison hidden in their food by guards. Orta believed all of this—from his arrest and incarceration to possible attempts on his life—was occurring because he had exposed the illegal actions of the police.

In April 2015, with protesters still rioting in New York and around the country about the decision not to indict Pantaleo, another recorded case of police brutality surfaced in the news. In North Charleston, South Carolina, video taken by Feidin Santana, a barber who had been walking to work, showed the end of a short scuffle between police officer Michael Slager and fifty-year-old Walter Scott. Slager had stopped Scott on the road for a broken brake light and later chased him down after Scott fled his vehicle. The video showed Scott and Slager briefly entangled with each other before Scott continued running. Slager then fired his weapon eight times at Scott's back, hitting him five times and killing him.

Unlike the video of Garner's death, Santana's recording proved instrumental in Slager's quick arrest, firing from the North Charleston police department, and indictment for first-degree murder. Santana later admitted that he had hesitated before making his video public because he feared police retribution for his actions.

In the wake of these and other high-profile manifestations of police brutality in 2014 and 2015, civil rights activists began calling on citizens to film any and all incidents of police misconduct they encountered. It is legal, they stated, to record police action in public places as long as police work is not interrupted. This legal allowance circulated throughout communities where citizens had reported that police had confiscated their cell phones at the scenes of alleged police misconduct and deleted video recordings.

To assist in recording incidents between citizens and police, the nonprofit American Civil Liberties Union (ACLU) collaborated with software developers to create the Mobile Justice application for smartphones. The app allows users to record videos of their encounters with police in case of any misconduct and refer to them when communicating with lawyers from local ACLU chapters. Other similar apps in development in 2015 would allow smartphone users to record and automatically upload videos of police brutality to YouTube and instantaneously alert the public, with text messages and live map technology, that they were being wrongfully arrested. The stated goal of these efforts is to increase citizen power over that of abusive police.

Opposing Viewpoints: Police Brutality scrutinizes issues related to police conduct in the United States. Authors offer various perspectives on these issues in chapters titled "Are Police Using Excessive Force?," "Is Police Brutality a Widespread Problem in the United States?," "How Can Police Brutality Be Stopped?," and "What Is the US Government's Response to Police Brutality?"

OPPOSING VIEWPOINTS® SERIES

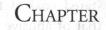
Are Police Using Excessive Force?

Chapter Preface

A merican police experienced a chaotic period in the mid-2010s. Multiple incidents across the United States in 2014 and 2015 left several African Americans dead at the hands of white police officers. In most cases, these deaths sparked violent protests, both in their respective cities and around the country. Rioters claimed that police brutality and racism were overtaking the United States. In Ferguson, Missouri—where eighteen-year-old Michael Brown was shot and killed by Darren Wilson, an officer in the city's police department—the question of excessive police force became a significant issue, especially after the US Justice Department concluded that, for years, Ferguson police had disproportionately targeted African Americans for searches and traffic stops, mostly to generate city revenue. In the midst of this, some news commentators began wondering whether the Fourth Amendment to the US Constitution, which bans unreasonable searches and seizures, still applied to the American people.

Founding father James Madison drew up the Fourth Amendment in 1789 as part of the Bill of Rights. Madison composed the Bill of Rights specifically to guard against the kinds of tyrannical offenses committed against the American colonists by the British. The Fourth Amendment was a prime example of this. It explicitly stated that the right of the American people to remain secure from unreasonable searches of themselves, their possessions, or their homes was not to be violated and that warrants to do so could not be issued against them without probable cause.

Madison conceived of this amendment when the memory of Great Britain's writs of assistance was still fresh in his mind. In the colonial era, to produce significant revenues for itself, Britain implemented numerous high taxes on American goods, intensely angering the colonists. To avoid paying these taxes, Americans began smuggling goods through a kind of black market. In response to this, King George III issued writs of assistance against the American people. These generalized search warrants allowed British soldiers to enter anyone's home or property at any time and begin searching for contraband, even when these searches were based on suspicion rather than on probable cause. The colonists were outraged by the writs of assistance, and when the Constitution was being created in the late 1780s, Madison ensured that the Fourth Amendment would forever protect Americans from such offenses.

The Fourth Amendment rose to prominence again in 2014 and 2015, when the US federal government confirmed that police in Ferguson, Missouri, had long been violating the constitutional rights of African Americans in the community. Attorney General Eric Holder, who led the investigation of the city, confirmed that Ferguson police consistently stopped and arrested residents without reasonable cause or suspicion and subsequently used unwarranted force against them. In addition, Holder's Justice Department report confirmed that Ferguson police had been targeting minorities for these unreasonable arrests based specifically on their race. Once this information was made known, the Ferguson Police Department faced scathing national criticism for its unlawful practices against African Americans.

The following chapter presents multiple viewpoints on the use of force by American police while carrying out their duties. Topics include the extent of police brutality, police racism against minorities, and police militarization.

> "Now, we must always consider the ex-
> cruciating possibility that when we call
> for help, we may well be summoning
> our own executioners."

Police Brutality Must Be Stopped

Richard Rowe

In the following viewpoint, Richard Rowe argues that American police officers have been abusing their power and that the country must take steps to stop this. He suggests, for example, removing officers' "trained observer" status so police testimony does not automatically outweigh that of others in court. Rowe believes that if all of his suggestions are followed, police will be able to return to their original purpose of protecting and serving. Rowe is a Florida-based writer.

As you read, consider the following questions:

1. How does Rowe argue against the claim that video cameras on police officers would be impractical?

2. What three results from a police officer's license plate information request does Rowe say could hurt suspected criminals when they encounter police?

3. According to Rowe, how much does a police officer make annually?

America's legal system is out of control. Not out of control in the sense that we can't do anything about it—only in that as a system, it has lost all control of itself.

It exists only to perpetuate its own existence, without strategic objective or goal. These days, stories of police brutality and abuses of power are so utterly rampant that it's almost become a sort of tragic cliché—like prison rape.

Yours truly has written no less than *three different stories* on police brutality *today alone*, with another one in the pipeline. Something must be done, and it somehow seems unlikely that any number of blog posts will do it—no matter how snarky, long-winded or ironic their hipster-esque self-references may be.

This issue is a highly complex one, an interconnected web of socioeconomic causalities spanning decades of graft, greed, racism and good old-fashioned political demagoguery. . . .

Revoke Officer *"Trained Observer"* Status

It might sound cute and fairly innocuous, but this anachronistic policy has sent more innocent people to prisons, hospitals and morgues than perhaps any other in history. That's why it's first on the list—and also because it's a near prerequisite for everything else. But what does *trained observer status* mean?

What it boils down to is this: If an officer says it happened, then it happened, because he's "trained to observe." Note the subtle difference between *"trained to observe"* and *"guaranteed not to lie."*

But in a courtroom, a police officer's word is literally law; even if a judge doesn't personally believe a word of what the

© Bill Schorr/Caglecartoons.com

cop says, he's bound by law to act as though he does. In the eyes of the law, this anachronism makes every police officer's eyes high-definition cameras, his ears radio telescopes, his nose the quality of a circling turkey vulture's and his memory as flawless as an MP3 player's.

But it doesn't make him *honest.*

If we're going to get anywhere at all, we have to accept that cops are humans, and humans will lie when it suits them. *Especially* when they know that lie will never be questioned. Can you think of many people who wouldn't? Putting on a uniform and jackboots doesn't change the basic morphology of the brain or basest parts of human nature. It only guarantees that when a human decides to act like an animal, he'll never be put in a cage.

The Mighty Glass Eye

Having read three paragraphs back, you probably already saw this one coming. If police can't be trusted to record things accurately, then what *can* we trust? Machines that are ... designed to record things accurately.

In this age of "*no pic, didn't happen,*" why is it that we're so slow to demand that cops provide proof? Once we revoke a police officer's *trained observer* status, his word is no better than anyone else's in court. But police by definition need a means of relaying information to the court; is it so insane a notion that we should use all technology at our disposal to provide that evidence?

Yes, 20 years ago, you could make a case that putting cameras and microphones on police officers was impractical. But that was when a "*small camcorder*" was the size and weight of a bag of dog food, and cost as much as a purebred Shih Tzu. Now, you can walk into any Walmart (or preferably Target) in the country and buy a video/audio recorder the size of a lighter with 12 hours of HD [high-definition] recording capacity for $200. The cheapest go for less than $20. So, the notion that it would be "*financially impractical*" to put cameras on cops is as utterly absurd an anachronism as *trained observer* status....

One technical point: Every officer should have four cameras ... four tiny glass eyes. One on their vest, two on a headset facing forward and backward, and a fourth "gun camera" on their service weapon set to start recording any time the weapon is out of its holster.

No pic, didn't happen.

Prerequisite Conviction for Resisting Arrest

One of the most maddening things about police brutality cases is how often the victims are arrested for "resisting arrest"—and *only* resisting arrest. Police know they have the power to hit anyone at any time with a felony for resisting arrest, whether they had reason to attempt arrest in the first place or not. Jails are full of people whose *only charge* is resisting arrest, or the adjunct "*failure to comply,*" or "*obstruction of justice.*"

Under the current system, a police officer could walk up to anyone on the street and tell them to put their hands out for cuffs. If the person asks them why, or in any way fails to immediately comply, the officer now hypothetically has grounds to arrest them for resisting arrest or failure to comply.

This abhorrent loophole effectively gives police carte blanche to throw anyone in jail, any time, whether they've committed a crime or not. And acquittals on these cases are extremely rare, because of *trained observer*. If the officer says you *"resisted arrest"* or *"failed to comply,"* you have de facto committed the crime for which he arrested you.

The system your author proposes is one of *prerequisite conviction* for any resisting arrest charge. Meaning that you must be convicted of the exact crime the officer charged you with during the attempted arrest *before* the state can press charges for resisting arrest. If there's no conviction for the original offense, there are no charges for *resisting arrest, failure to comply* or *obstruction of justice*. Period. . . .

Classify License Plate Information as Private

This might sound a bit pedantic, but it's more important than you might think.

Once you're in the system, you're in the system. If you've ever been arrested for possession of pot, been on probation, or had any interaction with law enforcement or jail, there's an extremely high probability of police harassment later.

Many modern police cars have cameras and software that automatically identify license plates, send the information request, and tell a police officer everything about you in real time. Typically including your picture, gender and race. And even police cars not equipped with this system have onboard computers that will give the same information almost as quickly.

This isn't just a problem for former foul criminals—especially not when you consider the degree and severity of racial profiling today. How high do you think the likelihood of "*smelling marijuana*" is if that computer displays a black face in Missouri or the name "Achmed" in Texas? Or if your name has too many vowels in Los Angeles? Or if you had a DUI [an arrest or conviction for driving under the influence] ten years ago in another state? The ability of officers to see your face and know everything about you without any just cause for knowing it does nothing but encourage harassment and profiling.

Your author will grant that some degree of identification is necessary; it's good to know if the person ahead of you has a warrant out for their arrest, an expired tag or a suspended driver's license. Fair enough. But that information can be vetted through a computer or dispatcher without sending all of your information to the officer. If you have a warrant or suspended license, green light to pull over, and here's the rest of the information. If not, mind your own business, officer.

The proposition here is simple: A cop has no right or reason to know who you are, what you're doing or what history you may have if they don't have cause to arrest or cite you. That doesn't change because you're driving down the street instead of walking down it. Personal information attached to your license plate through the DMV [Department of Motor Vehicles] should be protected against unreasonable search in the same way as all other forms of state or government identification. . . .

The "Special Duties" Amendment— They're Not "*Special*" Duties When They're Your *Job*

We saved this one for last because it may be the most important of all—official creation of a legal "*special duty*" amendment for police, either on the state or federal level.

Consider this: An entry-level soldier in the U.S. Army gets paid about $1,300 a month, while in boot camp, and about $16,800 a year afterward. For that, we get a person who flies off to exotic foreign lands to kill people, while those same people are on a daily basis trying to kill him with guns, bombs and rabid camels. For $16,800 a year, we get someone willing to endure hellish conditions for months or years at a time away from his family, while every single day waking up knowing it could be his last. And if not his, then maybe someone he knows. All for love of his country, and the pride of serving his community. All that, for under $16,800 a year.

The average police officer makes $47,623 a year—almost *three times* what a starting soldier makes.

Granted, out of that salary must come room, board and food. But that room is in their own home, with their own family, the board is their own comfortable bed, and the food (judging by the physique of the typical cop) is probably pretty well removed from the average soldier's K ration [food ration]. And then there are the perks, including a company car. Granted soldiers also get company cars, but those do have an awful tendency to get exploded with RPGs [rocket-propelled grenades] and IEDs [improvised explosive devices]. But soldiers accept that—it's part of the job we pay them to do.

So how is it that we've come to expect *less* of people we pay *three times more*?

As clearly as possible, absent the legal jargon, the basic nature of our proposed federal/state "*Special Duty*" amendment is as follows:

- An officer's primary job is to work toward the betterment of his/her community—the power to arrest people is a necessary component of that duty, but arresting members of the community is *not* the officer's primary function. . . .

- All members of all law enforcement organizations are expected to take any opportunity to risk their lives for *any* member of the community, be they rich or poor, black or white, or even a suspect in a crime. It is the officer's duty to treat all persons, even those they're arresting, as members of that community, subject to the same protection from harm as any other person. And yes, that includes protection from *other officers.*

- If an officer is accused of failing to perform in his *Special Duties*, he is to be placed before a jury of local community members. They, representing an economic and racial cross-section of that community, will decide if the officer has violated his "*special duties.*" If so, the officer is subject to termination and permanent barring of any future work in law enforcement.

ADDENDUM: Establishment of a national database for tracking cases of police use of force, suspected police brutality and racial profiling.

ADDENDUM 2: Establishment of a "*balance*" clause for hiring in police departments. Whatever the racial or ethnic makeup of the police jurisdiction may be, the police force should reflect that as closely as possible. If the community is 75 percent black, the police force should be as well. If it is 95 percent white, the police force should be.

Some Distant Future

Isn't it sad that it's come to this? Sadder still that we should even have to *say* it, to have to define the *concept* of a "public servant" to those very people.

There was a time when police officers were respected, even among the criminal community, as public servants. Cops were once our heroes, our icons and role models; they were the people we knew we could call on for help. They were the good guys . . . even the bad guys understood that cops risked their lives daily "*to protect and serve.*"

Now, we must always consider the excruciating possibility that when we call for help, we may well be summoning our own executioners.

For most of our nation's history, the death of a police officer was a tragedy. Now, it's mourned by law enforcement, but everyone else sheds a public tear, and shrugs a private shoulder. We've lost our love for law, or at least those who use it to protect us. We miss the simplicity (once so sadly taken for granted) of knowing that *the good guys* are never more than a phone call away.

We miss our heroes.

I believe that someday, in some distant future, we may get our heroes back. Certainly, this cycle of violence, brutality and injustice can't continue upward forever. I hope I live to see its zenith, and fall.

But, if you don't want to wait for it to fall on its own—here's your battle axe.

Start hacking.

> *"How common are such incidents of po-*
> *lice use of force, both lethal and non-*
> *lethal, in the United States? . . . The*
> *indisputable reality is that we do not*
> *fully know."*

There Is Conflicting Information on Police Brutality

John Wihbey

In the following viewpoint, John Wihbey contends that available data show mixed results with regard to police brutality in the United States. While some studies have shown that police officers generally use more force against minorities, Wihbey claims, other studies have shown that they do not. According to Wihbey, these results indicate that it is difficult to determine the national character of American police. Wihbey is a writer for Journalist's Resource, a project based at Harvard's Shorenstein Center on Media, Politics and Public Policy.

As you read, consider the following questions:

1. Among what two minority groups in particular does Wihbey say confidence in law enforcement is low?

2. According to Wihbey's research, what two factors have been linked to the decreased likelihood that a police officer will use force?

3. What does Wihbey say happened in Rialto, California, after that city's police department began wearing body cameras?

Allegations of the use of excessive force by U.S. police departments continue to generate headlines more than two decades after the 1992 Los Angeles riots brought the issue to mass public attention and spurred some law enforcement reforms.

On Staten Island, N.Y., the July 2014 death of Eric Garner because of the apparent use of a "choke hold" by an officer sparked outrage. A month later in Ferguson, Mo., the fatal shooting of teenager Michael Brown by officer Darren Wilson ignited protests, and a grand jury's decision not to indict Wilson triggered further unrest. In November, Tamir Rice was shot by police in Cleveland, Ohio. He was 12 years old and playing with a toy pistol. On April 4, 2015, Walter L. Scott was shot by a police officer after a routine traffic stop in North Charleston, S.C. The same month, Freddie Gray died while in police custody in Baltimore, setting off widespread unrest. The policeman in the South Carolina case, Michael T. Slager, was charged with murder based on a cell phone video. In Baltimore, the driver of the police van in which Gray died, Caesar Goodson, was charged with second-degree murder, with lesser charges for five other officers. There have been no indictments in the earlier cases.

These follow other recent incidents and controversies, including an April 2014 finding by the U.S. Department of Justice (DOJ), following a two-year investigation, that the Albu-querque, N.M., police department "engages in a pattern or practice of use of excessive force, including deadly force, in violation of the Fourth Amendment," and a similar DOJ find-ing in December 2014 with regard to the Cleveland police de-partment. In March 2015, the DOJ also issued a report detail-ing a pattern of "clear racial disparities" and "discriminatory intent" on the part of the Ferguson, Mo., police department.

The events of 2014–2015 have prompted further calls by some police officials, politicians and scholars for another round of national reforms, in order to better orient "police culture" toward democratic ideals.

Two Sides, Disparate Views

Surveys in recent years with minority groups—Latinos and African Americans, in particular—suggest that confidence in law enforcement is relatively low, and large portions of these communities believe police are likely to use excessive force on suspects. A 2014 Pew Research Center survey confirms stark racial divisions in response to the Ferguson police shooting, as well, while Gallup provides insights on historical patterns of distrust. According to a Pew/*USA Today* poll conducted in Au-gust 2014, Americans of all races collectively "give relatively low marks to police departments around the country for hold-ing officers accountable for misconduct, using the appropriate amount of force, and treating racial and ethnic groups equally." Social scientists who have done extensive field re-search and interviews note the deep sense of mistrust embed-ded in many communities.

Numerous efforts have been made by members of the law enforcement community to ameliorate these situations, in-cluding promising strategies such as "community policing." Still, from a police perspective, law enforcement in the United States continues to be dangerous work—America has a rela-tively higher homicide rate compared to other developed nations and has many more guns per capita. Citizens seldom learn of the countless incidents where officers choose to hold fire and display restraint under extreme stress. Some research has shown that even well-trained officers are not consistently able to fire their weapon in time before a suspect holding a gun can raise it and fire first; this makes split-second judgments, even under "ideal" circumstances, exceptionally difficult. But as the FBI [Federal Bureau of Investigation] points out, police departments and officers sometimes do not handle the aftermath of incidents well in terms of transparency and clarity, even when force was reasonably applied, fueling public confusion and anger.

In 2013, 49,851 officers were assaulted in the line of duty, with an injury rate of 29.2 percent, according to the FBI. Twenty-seven were murdered that year.

FBI Director: No "Reliable Grasp" of Problem

How common are such incidents of police use of force, both lethal and nonlethal, in the United States? Has there been progress in America? The indisputable reality is that we do not fully know. FBI director James B. Comey stated the following in a remarkable February 2015 speech:

> Not long after riots broke out in Ferguson late last summer, I asked my staff to tell me how many people shot by police were African American in this country. I wanted to see trends. I wanted to see information. They couldn't give it to me, and it wasn't their fault. Demographic data regarding officer-involved shootings is not consistently reported to us through our Uniform Crime Reporting Program. Because reporting is voluntary, our data is incomplete and therefore, in the aggregate, unreliable. . . .

Without a doubt, training for police has become more standardized and professionalized in recent decades. A 2008 paper in the *Northwestern University Law Review* provides useful background on the evolving legal and policy history relating to the use of force by police and the "reasonableness" standard by which officers are judged. Related jurisprudence is still being defined, most recently in the 2007 *Scott v. Harris* decision by the U.S. Supreme Court. But inadequate data and reporting—and the challenge of uniformly defining excessive versus justified force—make objective understanding of trends difficult.

For perhaps the best overall summary of police use-of-force issues, see "A Multi-method Evaluation of Police Use of Force Outcomes: Final Report to the National Institute of Justice," a 2010 study conducted by some of the nation's leading criminal justice scholars.

Available Statistics, Background on Use of Force

The Justice Department releases statistics on this and related issues, although these data sets are only periodically updated: It found that in 2008, among people who had contact with police, "an estimated 1.4% had force used or threatened against them during their most recent contact, which was not statistically different from the percentages in 2002 (1.5%) and 2005 (1.6%)." In terms of the volume of citizen complaints, the Justice Department also found that there were 26,556 complaints lodged in 2002; this translates to "33 complaints per agency and 6.6 complaints per 100 full-time sworn officers." However, "overall rates were higher among large municipal police departments, with 45 complaints per agency, and 9.5 complaints per 100 full-time sworn officers." In 2011, about 62.9 million people had contact with the police. . . .

As mentioned, the FBI does publish statistics on "justifiable homicide" by law enforcement officers: The data show that there have been about 400 such incidents nationwide each year. However, FiveThirtyEight, among other journalism outlets, has examined the potential problems with these figures. News investigations suggest that the rates of deadly force usage are far from uniform. For example, Los Angeles saw an increase in such incidents in 2011, while Massachusetts saw more officers firing their weapon over the period 2009–2013. . . .

A 2012 study in the *Criminal Justice Policy Review* analyzed the patterns of behavior of one large police department—more than 1,000 officers—and found that a "small proportion of officers are responsible for a large proportion of force incidents, and that officers who frequently use force differ in important and significant ways from officers who use force less often (or not at all)." A 2007 study in *Criminal Justice and Behavior*, "Police Education, Experience and the Use of Force," found that officers with more experience and education may be less likely to use force, while a review of case studies suggests that specific training programs and accountability structures can lower the use of violence by police departments.

Researchers continue to refine analytical procedures in order to make more accurate estimates based on police reports and other data.

Characteristics of Suspects

A widely publicized report in October 2014 by ProPublica, a leading investigative and data journalism outlet, concluded that young black males are 21 times more likely to be shot by police than their white counterparts: "The 1,217 deadly police shootings from 2010 to 2012 captured in the federal data show that blacks, age 15 to 19, were killed at a rate of 31.17 per million, while just 1.47 per million white males in that age range died at the hands of police."

Research has definitively established that "racial profiling" by law enforcement exists—that persons of color are more likely to be stopped by police. FBI director James Comey's 2015 comments are again relevant here:

Police Are Racist and Violent

As a kid, I got used to being stopped by the police. I grew up in an inner-ring suburb of St. Louis. It was the kind of place where officers routinely roughed up my friends and family for no good reason. . . .

But I knew police weren't all bad. One of my father's closest friends was a cop. He became a mentor to me and encouraged me to join the force. He told me that I could use the police's power and resources to help my community.

So in 1994, I joined the St. Louis Police Department. I quickly realized how naive I'd been. I was floored by the dysfunctional culture I encountered.

I won't say all, but many of my peers were deeply racist.

One example: A couple of officers ran a website called St. Louis Coptalk, where officers could post about their experience and opinions. At some point during my career, it became so full of racist rants that the site administrator temporarily shut it down. Cops routinely called anyone of color a "thug," whether they were the victim or just a bystander. . . .

Unfortunately, I don't think better training alone will reduce police brutality. . . . The problem is that cops aren't held accountable for their actions, and they know it. These officers violate rights with impunity. They know there's a different criminal justice system for civilians and police.

Redditt Hudson,
"Being a Cop Showed Me Just How Racist
and Violent the Police Are. There's Only One Fix,"
Washington Post, *December 6, 2014.*

[P]olice officers on patrol in our nation's cities often work in environments where a hugely disproportionate percentage of street crime is committed by young men of color. Something happens to people of goodwill working in that environment. After years of police work, officers often can't help but be influenced by the cynicism they feel.

A mental shortcut becomes almost irresistible and maybe even rational by some lights. The two young black men on one side of the street look like so many others the officer has locked up. Two white men on the other side of the street—even in the same clothes—do not. The officer does not make the same association about the two white guys, whether that officer is white or black. And that drives different behavior. The officer turns toward one side of the street and not the other. We need to come to grips with the fact that this behavior complicates the relationship between police and the communities they serve.

While the cases of Rodney King in 1991 and Amadou Diallo in 1999 heightened the country's awareness of race and policing, research has not uniformly corroborated the contention that minorities are more likely, on average, to be subject to acts of police force than are whites. A 2010 paper published in the *Southwest Journal of Criminal Justice* reviewed more than a decade's worth of peer-reviewed studies and found that while many studies established a correlation between minority status and police use of force, many other studies did not—and some showed mixed results. . . .

Potential Impact of Body Cameras

Video recordings of interactions between the police and the public have increased significantly in recent years as technology has improved and the number of distribution channels has expanded. Any standard smartphone can now make a video—as was the case in the Walter L. Scott shooting—and dash-mounted cameras in police cars have become increasingly common.

The mandatory adoption of body cameras by police has been suggested to increase transparency in interactions between law enforcement officials and the public. A 2014 study from the U.S. Department of Justice, "Police Officer Body-Worn Cameras: Assessing the Evidence," reviews available research on the costs and benefits of body-worn camera technology. The author, Michael D. White of Arizona State University, identified five empirical studies on body cameras and assessed their conclusions. In particular, a year after the Rialto, Calif., police department began requiring all officers to wear body cameras, use of force by officers fell by 60% and citizen complaints dropped by nearly 90%. The researcher notes:

> The decline in complaints and use of force may be tied to improved citizen behavior, improved police officer behavior, or a combination of the two. It may also be due to changes in citizen complaint reporting patterns (rather than a civilizing effect), as there is evidence that citizens are less likely to file frivolous complaints against officers wearing cameras. Available research cannot disentangle these effects; thus, more research is needed. . . .

Public Opinion and the Press

The coverage of such incidents by mass media has been studied by researchers, some of whom have concluded that the press has often distorted and helped justify questionable uses of force. Finally, survey data continue to confirm the existence of undercurrents of racism and bias in America, despite demonstrable social progress; a 2014 Stanford [University] study shows how awareness of higher levels of black incarceration can prompt greater support among whites for tougher policing and prison programs.

> *"Tens of thousands of law-abiding mi-*
> *norities endured police searches based*
> *solely on their skin color."*

Police Are Racist Against Minorities

Linn Washington Jr.

In the following viewpoint, Linn Washington Jr. argues that America's police disproportionately target minorities for use of force. This is proven, he writes, in cities such as Philadelphia, where the police stop and frisk more blacks than whites. Washington wonders whether the United States ever intends to address this systemic racism in its police forces. Washington is a contributor to ThisCantBeHappening.net, an online news outlet.

As you read, consider the following questions:

1. According to Washington, why have efforts to implement civilian oversight over police unions been unsuccessful?

2. According to Washington, what decision of President Lyndon Johnson's did Martin Luther King Jr. say undermined the United States' efforts to fight poverty?

3. What does Washington say the US Justice Department discovered about the Ferguson Police Department following an investigation?

The report released in early March [2015] by a panel President [Barack] Obama appointed to examine serious shortcomings in police practices across America, including the shooting of unarmed people, mostly nonwhite, listed problems and proposed solutions that are hauntingly similar to those found in a report on police abuses released 47 years ago by another presidential panel.

Distant Parallels

The March 1968 report of the presidential panel popularly known as the Kerner Commission noted with dismay that many minorities nationwide regarded police as "an occupying force"—a presence that generated fear, not feelings of security.

The March 2015 report from President Obama's panel made a similar finding, noting that perceptions of police as an "occupying force coming in from the outside to rule and control the community" had sabotaged the ability of law enforcement to build trust in many communities.

Reactions to police brutality, particularly fatal encounters, triggered protests and riots that sparked both President Barack Obama and President Lyndon Johnson almost two generations earlier to appoint these two panels.

Sadly, the recommendations from President Obama's panel could sink under the weight of the same forces that sank full implementation of the Kerner Commission proposals: systemic recalcitrance from all sectors of American society to reforms devised to remediate festering race-based inequities.

The Obama panel recommended "civilian oversight of law enforcement," calling this step essential to "strengthen trust with the community." The Kerner Commission report had similarly called for the establishment of "fair mechanisms to redress grievances" against police.

However, for decades, police unions, backed by "law-and-order" politicians in city councils, state legislatures, and Congress, have vigorously opposed independent oversight by civilians and even oversight from governmental entities.

Such opposition mounted by America's national police union—the Fraternal Order of Police [FOP]—early last year killed Obama's nomination of a civil rights lawyer to head the US Justice Department's [USJD's] Civil Rights Division. The national FOP in that case made it clear it resented any Justice Department monitoring of state and local police practices. Despite patterns of police misconduct that had led to what was at best only infrequent Justice Department monitoring, US senators—Republicans and Democrats—backed the national police union's opposition to Obama's nominee.

The Kerner Commission, which had examined race-based inequities beyond police brutality, called for a massive influx of resources to tackle poverty and discrimination.

That proposal from President Johnson's panel, formally titled the National Advisory Commission on Civil Disorders because it was a wave of riots and uprisings in cities across the country in the 1960s that led to its creation, prompted immediate opposition from conservatives. Resources being poured into the war in Vietnam further doomed that proposal.

Dr. Martin Luther King Jr., during the year before his April 1968 assassination, stridently criticized conservatives for failing to forthrightly attack poverty, and he blasted President Johnson for channeling increasing resources to the Vietnam War, which then shortchanged Johnson's programs to address poverty. King had blasted police brutality twice during his seminal "I Have a Dream" speech in 1963.

A Disproportionate Impact

Sound familiar?

Institutional Racism

In the wake of the protests following a grand jury's failure to indict [white police officer] Darren Wilson for killing [black teenager] Michael Brown, President Obama met Monday [in December 2014] with civil rights leaders and, separately, with a group of young activist leaders and told them that the task at hand is to initiate a "sustained conversation" that addresses the "simmering distrust that exists between too many police departments and too many communities of color."

Two days later, a grand jury in New York City failed to indict the white police officer whose choke hold killed Eric Garner as bystanders taped the incident. . . .

Black men are not dying at the hands of (mostly) white cops—nor are those cops being excused from legal responsibility—because of mutual distrust between black and brown people and law enforcement agencies. To suggest so simply, and perhaps deliberately, mistakes the symptom for the disease.

Trust, or lack thereof, is based on lived experience, and it is the actions of law enforcement in communities of color that have eroded black and brown Americans' trust. To present the situation as mutual distrust not only obscures the specific causes of that distrust—it intimates that everyone is equally responsible for the problem. . . .

Our political leaders should not begin to offer solutions for a problem if they won't even name it: systemic, institutional racism exists in police forces throughout our country.

Vincent Warren,
"The Real Problem in Ferguson, New York
and All of America Is Institutional Racism,"
Guardian, *December 4, 2014.*

One proposal from Obama's panel, formally known as the Task Force on 21st Century Policing, called for initiatives "that address the core issues of poverty, education, health and safety." This panel pointed out the persistently ignored reality that the "justice system alone cannot solve many of the under-lying conditions that give rise to crime." Clouding chances of federal funding increases to fight poverty is the fact that con-servatives controlling Capitol Hill have consistently blocked Obama's modest anti-poverty proposals.

One core yet consistently downplayed dynamic driving in-action on police abuses is the refusal of too many Americans to acknowledge the reality that police brutality exists and that it disproportionately impacts minorities.

A survey conducted by the 2015 Obama panel found that 72 percent of whites felt police treated blacks and whites equally while 62 percent of blacks felt they received unequal (and unjust) treatment from police.

The 1968 Kerner report declared that abrasive relations between police and minority groups "have been a major source of grievance, tension, and ultimately disorder."

The Kerner report found that police abuses were a key fac-tor leading to most of the 24 riots it studied in 23 cities. A quarter of a century later, not much had changed. America's most destructive riot, the 1992 eruption in Los Angeles fol-lowing the acquittal of four white policemen charged in the videotaped beating of black motorist Rodney King, caused 53 deaths and over $1 billion in property damage. Another 22 years later, the riots in Ferguson, Missouri, last summer erupted in the wake of the fatal shooting of unarmed black teen Michael Brown by a white policeman.

The refusal of either state or federal authorities to file any charges against the officer who fatally gunned down Brown underscored what the 1968 Kerner Commission stated was a "widespread belief" among blacks that a "double standard of justice" existed in America.

Profiling and Discrimination

Another factor in the persistence of police abuses is the failure of authorities to practice what they preach.

The Obama panel called for the adoption and enforcement of policies "prohibiting profiling and discrimination"—a suggestion long ignored by Obama panel co-chair Charles Ramsey, the police commissioner in Philadelphia. Yet, Ramsey's department has been stopping and frisking mostly young black men, and resisting changes to that tactic, for his entire tenure in Philadelphia.

A report issued by the Pennsylvania ACLU [American Civil Liberties Union] just days before release of the Obama panel's interim report faulted Philadelphia police for targeting blacks in that city's controversial stop-and-frisk campaign, which is the prime anti-crime initiative of Philadelphia's mayor, Michael Nutter, an African American like Ramsey.

Philadelphia police under Ramsey's command targeted blacks for 72 percent of stops and 80 percent of frisks of pedestrians during one six-month period in 2014, according to that ACLU report monitoring the PPD's [Philadelphia Police Department's] poor compliance with a 2011 federal court consent decree meant to end racist profiling.

In over 95 percent of all frisks in Philadelphia during the 2014 review period, the ACLU report stated, police recovered neither weapons nor drugs. That low recovery of contraband meant that tens of thousands of law-abiding minorities endured police searches based solely on their skin color.

A recent US Justice Department report found police in Ferguson unfairly targeted blacks for enforcement in part to produce court fines to fuel the city budget of Ferguson. "The harms of Ferguson's police and court practices are borne disproportionately by African Americans and there is evidence that this is due in part to intentional discrimination on the basis of race," the USJD report stated.

Obama's panel, like the Kerner Commission before it, has provided some palpable proposals for moving away from repressive and racist policing. However, the question remains: Does America have the will or even the desire to attack racism and lawlessness within law enforcement?

> *"Police officers on patrol in our nation's cities often work in environments where a hugely disproportionate percentage of street crime is committed by young men of color."*

Police Are Not Racist Against Minorities

James B. Comey

In the following viewpoint, James B. Comey contends that even though national data about racial discrimination among police are inconclusive, police officers are mostly good people who fall into the mental shortcuts that lead to racism. A large percentage of street crime, Comey claims, is committed by minorities. The police then naturally develop patterns of judging individuals from minority groups before they know anything about them. Comey is director of the Federal Bureau of Investigation (FBI).

As you read, consider the following questions:

1. According to Comey, what makes it easy for law enforcement to assume all suspects they arrest are lying?

James B. Comey, "Hard Truths: Law Enforcement and Race," Federal Bureau of Investigation, February 12, 2015. Courtesy of FBI.

2. What does Comey suggest doing to help minorities avoid police encounters?

3. What does Comey say American citizens should do to respect the work of police officers?

Thank you, President [John J.] DeGioia. And good morning, ladies and gentlemen. Thank you for inviting me to Georgetown University. I am honored to be here. I wanted to meet with you today [February 12, 2015], as President DeGioia said, to share my thoughts on the relationship between law enforcement and the diverse communities we serve and protect. Like a lot of things in life, that relationship is complicated. Relationships often are.

Beautiful Healy Hall—part of, and all around where we sit now—was named after this great university's 29th president, Patrick Francis Healy. Healy was born into slavery, in Georgia, in 1834. His father was an Irish immigrant plantation owner and his mother, a slave. Under the laws of that time, Healy and his siblings were considered to be slaves. Healy is believed to be the first African American to earn a PhD, the first to enter the Jesuit order, and the first to be president of Georgetown University or any predominantly white university.

Given Georgetown's remarkable history, and that of President Healy, this struck me as an appropriate place to talk about the difficult relationship between law enforcement and the communities we are sworn to serve and protect.

With the death of Michael Brown in Ferguson [Missouri], the death of Eric Garner in Staten Island [New York], the ongoing protests throughout the country, and the assassinations of NYPD [New York City Police Department] officers Wenjian Liu and Rafael Ramos, we are at a crossroads. As a society, we can choose to live our everyday lives, raising our families and going to work, hoping that someone, somewhere, will do something to ease the tension—to smooth over the conflict. We can roll up our car windows, turn up the radio and drive around these problems, or we can choose to have an open and honest discussion about what our relationship is today—what it should be, what it could be, and what it needs to be—if we took more time to better understand one another.

Current Issues Facing Law Enforcement

Unfortunately, in places like Ferguson and New York City, and in some communities across this nation, there is a disconnect between police agencies and many citizens—predominantly in communities of color.

Serious debates are taking place about how law enforcement personnel relate to the communities they serve, about the appropriate use of force, and about real and perceived biases, both within and outside of law enforcement. These are important debates. Every American should feel free to express an informed opinion—to protest peacefully, to convey frustration and even anger in a constructive way. That's what makes our democracy great. Those conversations—as bumpy and uncomfortable as they can be—help us understand different perspectives and better serve our communities. Of course, these are only conversations in the true sense of that word if we are willing not only to talk but to listen, too.

I worry that this incredibly important and incredibly difficult conversation about race and policing has become focused entirely on the nature and character of law enforcement officers when it should also be about something much harder to discuss. Debating the nature of policing is very important, but I worry that it has become an excuse, at times, to avoid doing something harder. . . .

The Truth

There is a reason that I require all new agents and analysts to study the FBI's interaction with Dr. Martin Luther King Jr. and to visit his memorial in Washington as part of their training. And there is a reason I keep on my desk a copy of Attorney General Robert Kennedy's approval of J. Edgar Hoover's request to wiretap Dr. King. It is a single page. The entire application is five sentences long; it is without fact or substance and is predicated on the naked assertion that there is "communist influence in the racial situation." The reason I do those things is to ensure that we remember our mistakes and that we learn from them.

One reason we cannot forget our law enforcement legacy is that the people we serve and protect cannot forget it, either. So we must talk about our history. It is a hard truth that lives on.

A second hard truth: Much research points to the widespread existence of unconscious bias. Many people in our white-majority culture have unconscious racial biases and react differently to a white face than a black face. In fact, we all, white and black, carry various biases around with us. I am reminded of the song from the Broadway hit *Avenue Q*: "Everyone's a Little Bit Racist." Part of it goes like this:

Look around and you will find

No one's really color blind.

Maybe it's a fact

We all should face

Everyone makes judgments

Based on race.

You should be grateful I did not try to sing that.

But if we can't help our latent biases, we can help our behavior in response to those instinctive reactions, which is why we work to design systems and processes that overcome that very human part of us all. Although the research may be unsettling, it is what we do next that matters most.

But racial bias isn't epidemic in law enforcement any more than it is epidemic in academia or the arts. In fact, I believe law enforcement overwhelmingly attracts people who want to do good for a living—people who risk their lives because they want to help other people. They don't sign up to be cops in New York or Chicago or L.A. to help white people or black people or Hispanic people or Asian people. They sign up because they want to help all people. And they do some of the hardest, most dangerous policing to protect people of color.

But that leads me to my third hard truth: Something happens to people in law enforcement. Many of us develop different flavors of cynicism that we work hard to resist because they can be lazy mental shortcuts. For example, criminal suspects routinely lie about their guilt, and nearly everybody we charge is guilty. That makes it easy for some folks in law enforcement to assume that everybody is lying and that no suspect, regardless of their race, could be innocent. Easy, but wrong.

Likewise, police officers on patrol in our nation's cities often work in environments where a hugely disproportionate percentage of street crime is committed by young men of color. Something happens to people of goodwill working in that environment. After years of police work, officers often can't help but be influenced by the cynicism they feel.

A mental shortcut becomes almost irresistible and maybe even rational by some lights. The two young black men on one side of the street look like so many others the officer has locked up. Two white men on the other side of the street—even in the same clothes—do not. The officer does not make the same association about the two white guys, whether that officer is white or black. And that drives different behavior. The officer turns toward one side of the street and not the other. We need to come to grips with the fact that this behavior complicates the relationship between police and the communities they serve.

So why has that officer—like his colleagues—locked up so many young men of color? Why does he have that life-shaping experience? Is it because he is a racist? Why are so many black men in jail? Is it because cops, prosecutors, judges, and juries are racist? Because they are turning a blind eye to white robbers and drug dealers?

The answer is a fourth hard truth: I don't think so. If it were so, that would be easier to address. We would just need to change the way we hire, train, and measure law enforcement and that would substantially fix it. We would then go get those white criminals we have been ignoring. But the truth is significantly harder than that.

The truth is that what really needs fixing is something only a few, like President [Barack] Obama, are willing to speak about, perhaps because it is so daunting a task. Through the "My Brother's Keeper" initiative, the president is addressing the disproportionate challenges faced by young men of color. For instance, data show that the percentage of young men not working or not enrolled in school is nearly twice as high for blacks as it is for whites. This initiative, and others like it, is about doing the hard work to grow drug-resistant and violence-resistant kids, especially in communities of color, so they never become part of that officer's life experience.

So many young men of color become part of that officer's life experience because so many minority families and communities are struggling, so many boys and young men grow up in environments lacking role models, adequate education, and decent employment—they lack all sorts of opportunities that most of us take for granted. A tragedy of American life—one that most citizens are able to drive around because it doesn't touch them—is that young people in "those neighborhoods" too often inherit a legacy of crime and prison. And with that inheritance, they become part of a police officer's life and shape the way that officer—whether white or black—sees the world. Changing that legacy is a challenge so enor-

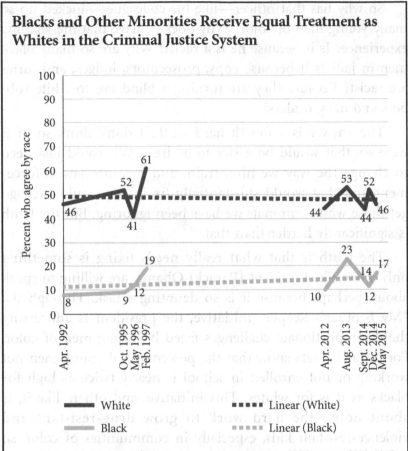

Blacks and Other Minorities Receive Equal Treatment as Whites in the Criminal Justice System

Sources: ABC News/Washington Post surveys, 1992–2012; PRRI surveys, 2013–2015.

TAKEN FROM: "Survey | Deep Divide Between Black and White Americans on Criminal Justice System's Racial Equality; Persists from Rodney King to Freddie Gray," Public Religion Research Institute, May 7, 2015.

mous and so complicated that it is, unfortunately, easier to talk only about the cops. And that's not fair. . . .

Seeing in Both Directions

We must work—in the words of New York City police commissioner Bill Bratton—to really see each other. Perhaps the reason we struggle as a nation is because we've come to see only what we represent, at face value, instead of who we are. We simply must see the people we serve.

But the "seeing" needs to flow in both directions. Citizens also need to really see the men and women of law enforcement. They need to see what police see through the windshields of their squad cars or as they walk down the street. They need to see the risks and dangers law enforcement officers encounter on a typical late-night shift. They need to understand the difficult and frightening work they do to keep us safe. They need to give them the space and respect to do their work, well and properly.

If they take the time to do that, what they will see are officers who are human, who are overwhelmingly doing the right thing for the right reasons, and who are too often operating in communities—and facing challenges—most of us choose to drive around. . . .

Not long after riots broke out in Ferguson late last summer, I asked my staff to tell me how many people shot by police were African American in this country. I wanted to see trends. I wanted to see information. They couldn't give it to me, and it wasn't their fault. Demographic data regarding officer-involved shootings is not consistently reported to us through our Uniform Crime Reporting Program. Because reporting is voluntary, our data is incomplete and therefore, in the aggregate, unreliable.

I recently listened to a thoughtful big-city police chief express his frustration with that lack of reliable data. He said he didn't know whether the Ferguson police shot one person a week, one a year, or one a century and that in the absence of good data, "all we get are ideological thunderbolts, when what we need are ideological agnostics who use information to try to solve problems." He's right. . . .

America isn't easy. America takes work. Today, February 12, is Abraham Lincoln's birthday. He spoke at Gettysburg

[Civil War battlefield in Pennsylvania] about a "new birth of freedom" because we spent the first four score and seven years of our history with fellow Americans held as slaves—President Healy, his siblings, and his mother among them. We have spent the 150 years since Lincoln spoke making great progress, but along the way treating a whole lot of people of color poorly. And law enforcement was often part of that poor treatment. That's our inheritance as law enforcement, and it is not all in the distant past. . . .

We simply must speak to each other honestly about all these hard truths.

In the words of Dr. King, "We must learn to live together as brothers or we will all perish together as fools."

We all have work to do—hard work, challenging work—and it will take time. We all need to talk and we all need to listen, not just about easy things, but about hard things, too. Relationships are hard. Relationships require work. So let's begin that work. It is time to start seeing one another for who and what we really are. Peace, security, and understanding are worth the effort. Thank you for listening to me today.

> "The presence of enough artillery to support the defense needs of a small nation would not be possible without an American ideology of state power at home and abroad."

Police Militarization Is a Problem in America

Carolyn Davis

In the following viewpoint, Carolyn Davis argues that police militarization is a serious problem in America. The extreme firepower of American police forces, she writes, symbolizes enthusiastic statist aggression exacerbated by racial biases. Davis contends that it is this racial inequality that makes police militarization unnecessary. Davis is a Methodist minister and a contributor to the Feminist Wire, a website focusing on critiques of sociopolitical and cultural issues.

As you read, consider the following questions:

1. In addition to police militarization, what two other police-related problems does Davis say are part of a larger issue in America?

2. What police offenses does Davis say compound the problem of advancing state power without public revolt?

3. According to Davis, what primarily drives the continuation of America's prison industrial complex?

Last year, I sat in front of my television in Brookline, a Boston suburb, and watched on live TV as police officers rolled armored vehicles down the streets of neighboring Watertown. Many officers were outfitted in tactical gear fit for urban warfare. They swarmed residential streets, assuming sniper positions atop cars and roofs. Others swept through homes, guns raised. When [2013 Boston Marathon bombing] suspect Dzhokhar Tsarnaev was finally found in a local resident's dry-docked boat—wounded and curled in the fetal position—police strafed the boat with gunfire. Bullets lodged in the boat and also in neighboring homes. Tsarnaev was later found not to have fired a single shot in that final exchange. In the short term, most of us felt relief. However, the sheer firepower exhibited by local police that day has continued to trouble me.

Advanced Military Units

Images coming out of Ferguson [Missouri, where a white police officer shot and killed an eighteen-year-old, unarmed black man in August 2014] in recent days have again revealed the vast capacities of modern police forces to rival advanced military units in tactical gear. And we have seen as well the psychotropic powers of such scenarios. Civilian police forces seem increasingly imbued with a sense that they are engaged in urban warfare against enemy combatants. In Ferguson, the contrast is especially stark: a predominantly white police force, dressed for combat and armed to the teeth, facing off against predominantly black citizens and protestors.

Recent commentaries from Talking Points Memo editor Josh Marshall and Patheos.com contributor Dan Arel have sought to separate the discourses of police militarization from racist policing practices. Both authors worry that conflating the two obscures and/or dismisses the long American history of racist police brutality. Their concerns are apt. In Ferguson, police outfitted in tactical fatigues atop armored vehicles aim guns at an unarmed black citizenry standing in protest. Such a confrontation embodies a volatile combination of racism and excess power that infects local police forces across the country. Yet, I suspect, there is a more nuanced connection between racism and police militarization in the United States that demands our engagement.

How and why did we come to unquestioningly welcome tactical police gear and armored vehicles on our city streets? The presence of enough artillery to support the defense needs of a small nation would not be possible without an American ideology of state power at home and abroad. Indeed, the hyper-aggression of police in Ferguson and elsewhere would not be possible without state power gained through racist micro-aggressions that pervade American life.

The violence in Ferguson reveals the intersection of several issues typically compartmentalized in public discourse. We often consider the rise of the prison industrial complex, racism and brutality in law enforcement and the militarization of civilian police departments as distinct issues. However, Ferguson makes clear the need for these phenomena to be examined as expressions of a larger problem. The situation in Ferguson has incited a powerful moment for the American conscience.

Overwhelming force against an unarmed citizenry can wake us up, especially when it is in our own backyard. But the compounding effects of so many stop-and-frisks, unwarranted traffic stops, questionable searches and seizures, rampant incarceration, and everyday oppressions make it possible to incrementally advance a consolidated sense of unified (white) state power without public revolt. The establishment of a docile citizenry is relatively easy to achieve when white folks believe they sit comfortably on the right side of state aggression.

America's Militarized Police

The weapons used in the "war on terror" that destroyed Afghanistan and Iraq have made their way to local law enforcement. While police forces across the country began a process of militarization complete with SWAT [special weapons and tactics] teams and flash-bang grenades when President [Ronald] Reagan intensified the "war on drugs," the post-9/11 [referring to the September 11, 2001, terrorist attacks on the United States] "war on terror" has added fuel to the fire.

Through laws and regulations like a provision in defense budgets that authorize the Pentagon to transfer surplus military gear to police forces, local law enforcement are using weapons found on the battlefields of South Asia and the Middle East.

A recent *New York Times* article by Matt Apuzzo reported that in the [Barack] Obama era, "police departments have received tens of thousands of machine guns; nearly 200,000 ammunition magazines; thousands of pieces of camouflage and night-vision equipment; and hundreds of silencers, armored cars and aircraft." . . .

The American Civil Liberties Union (ACLU) brought more attention to police militarization when it issued a comprehensive, nearly 100-page (appendix and endnotes included) report. . . . The ACLU concluded that "American policing has become excessively militarized through the use of weapons and tactics designed for the battlefield" and that this militarization "unfairly impacts people of color and undermines individual liberties, and it has been allowed to happen in the absence of any meaningful public discussion."

Alex Kane, "11 Shocking Facts About America's Militarized Police Forces," AlterNet, June 27, 2014.

A System of Racism

Militarization of police units is also deeply enmeshed with the rise of a prison industrial complex that relies on early and repeat incarceration of society's disenfranchised. Many Americans are unwilling to challenge a system that quietly funnels a staggering number of black men into its machinations. Policing and sentencing laws destroy the capacity of so many black youths to escape cycles of petty crime and drastic sentences. Unsurprisingly, at the system's heart is profit: privatized prison contractors who benefit from increasingly high rates of recidivism. The system profits significantly from exploiting entrenched (and yet unproven) beliefs about deterrence and rehabilitation.

An armored police force is not necessary in such a system of pervasive racism and structural inequality. But police militarization can become a 'logical' extension of state operations, particularly where ideology needs shoring up.

American foreign policy echoes confidence in the capacity (and authority) of the state to exert disproportionate force for deterrence and social rehabilitation. Such ideology feeds on ideals of social purity, moral righteousness, and firm boundaries between enemies and allies. It is the same ideology that has empowered increasingly armed police to carry out racist and mortally dangerous policing practices at the expense of basic civil liberties. When this doctrine is turned outward, we drive tanks through the streets of Baghdad [Iraq]. Turned inward, we drive tanks through the streets of Watertown and Ferguson.

The notion of the American military as a global police force is a natural complement to domestic "values," including profit. The rise of nation building as a foreign policy doctrine has proved profitable for defense and military contractors. We are remiss not to recognize the role of profit and privatization in American police militarization as well. Weapons and defense contractors benefit from stoking the hyper-vigilance of the modern police force, outfitting American police units while enjoying the excesses of Defense Department contracts.

Meanwhile, many of us continue to live in the in-between, especially if we are white. Many Americans are generally privileged to enjoy neither the regular and racialized threat of police intimidation and incarceration nor the receiving end of troubling foreign policy (or a rocket). In the wake of Ferguson, we must redouble our efforts to raise questions about the links between racism, power, and the state. Speaking of armored vehicles and racist policing is not an either/or proposition but rather a deeply enmeshed problem for the modern state.

> *"Far too often, the cops find themselves in need of the 'big guns' and body armor."*

Public Safety Requires Police Militarization

Jazz Shaw

In the following viewpoint, Jazz Shaw contends that the militarization of the United States' police forces is necessary for law enforcement officers to perform their duties. Police should never find themselves outmatched by criminals, Shaw believes, and therefore should always maintain the level of firepower truly required to protect and serve their communities. Shaw is a contributor to Hot Air, *a conservative political blog.*

As you read, consider the following questions:

1. What does Shaw say should be a sign that police militarization is not inherently bad?

2. According to Shaw, what does the left say about protecting schools from gun violence?

3. What does Shaw say is a good reason for America to retain its militarized police forces?

The rioting, protests and controversy continue to swirl around Ferguson [Missouri, where police officer Darren Wilson shot Michael Brown, an eighteen-year-old, unarmed black man in August 2014] this weekend, and you will no doubt be reading plenty of coverage from both sides about it. But in the background, a disturbing, larger national conversation has erupted out of the troubles in the St. Louis suburb. The hot topic everywhere seems to be a growing call to halt the so called "militarization" of the nation's civilian police forces, highlighted by the riot suppression gear on display in Ferguson. It's an argument coming from both sides of the ideological spectrum, too.

The *IBD* [*Investor's Business Daily*] editorial board warns us to "beware" of this trend. John Fund, writing at *National Review*, worries over not just police but a host of federal agencies being armed to the teeth. Bob Barr [lawyer and former member of the US House of Representatives] sounds the alarm as to how the psyche of our police must become warped when they are equipped like soldiers. Our own Noah Rothman has written thoughtfully on the subject, expressing some of his own concerns.

A Rush to Defang the Police

Frankly, I find the whole discussion to be a rather rapid rush to judgment and lacking in larger context. As far as the specific incidents in Ferguson go, we still need a lot more information before final conclusions can be drawn. The details of the initial shooting may remain in question, but what followed was well documented. Riots and looting broke out on a massive scale for such a small town and continue this morning. The local police stood on the edge of being completely overwhelmed. And whether or not you find their level of response appropriate, this one local disturbance has turned into a national demand to defang the police. The *Washington Post* quickly began issuing advice on how to tame the cops. Clearly the nation's legislators were listening, as Hank Johnson (D-Georgia) has already drafted legislation to do just that.

Am I the only one who finds this rather insulting to the nation's first responders in general? Even if we are to assume that the Ferguson police crossed a line in breaking out their heaviest equipment in an attempt to reestablish control (which has not been conclusively proven at all, in my opinion), what of the rest of the country? As these critics frequently note, police departments in cities and towns of all sizes have been equipped with more modern, military-style equipment for quite some time now, and they don't seem to be converting the rest of the nation into a series of oppressive death camps. And far too often, the cops find themselves in need of the "big guns" and body armor.

In case you think I'm coming in late to this debate, it's not true. There was apparently a meeting held at some point in which Radley Balko was appointed as the go-to guy for such discussions, but that dates back quite a ways. More than a year ago, Balko was pushing his ideas about so-called "warrior cops" and at that time I penned an editorial stating that he was going too far.

> Do we need "kinder and gentler" cops interacting with the community in a friendly fashion? It is certainly to the benefit of the police to be in good standing with a cooperative community and to know the people they protect and serve, but they also deserve a fighting chance when the situation suddenly turns violent and ugly. The rise of "warrior cops" may not be what everyone would hope for, but I don't see any realistic alternatives.

New Changes for New Times

While I both understand and sympathize with the reminiscing for the good old days, the times have changed. The era of the

Police Militarization Is Needed

St. Louis County's top police officer said ... that the heavy-armored trucks and some of the military-style equipment used by police in last month's [August 2014] unrest in Ferguson [Missouri] helped keep civilians and law enforcement officers safe.

Col. Jon Belmar's defense comes as the actions of his officers in Ferguson have been broadly criticized and spurred a national debate about the militarization of local law enforcement agencies. The military buildup began after the federal government doled out increased funding in the wake of the Sept. 11 [2001] attacks.

"I think we have to look at this from another vantage point," said Belmar, in an interview with *USA Today* after addressing 200 top law enforcement officers from across the country gathered in Chicago by the Police Executive Research Forum.

"Had we not had the ability to protect officers with those vehicles, I am afraid that we would have to engage people with our own gunfire. I really think having the armor gave us the ability not to have pulled one trigger....
I think the military uses armor to be able to provide an offensive force, and police departments use trucks like that so they don't have to."

St. Louis County Police Department led the law enforcement response during the first week of protests following the shooting death of unarmed teenager Michael Brown.

Aamer Madhani,
"St. Louis County Chief Defends Militarization of Police,"
USA Today, *September 16, 2014.*

lovable flatfoot, twirling his baton and wagging a finger at the precocious kid about to steal some penny candy has passed us by. Have we collectively forgotten the riots that took place following the Rodney King verdict?[1] How about the now infamous North Hollywood shootout?[2] And for our friends on the left, what about the next time somebody goes into an elementary school armed with a Bushmaster [assault rifle] and a couple of 9mm Glocks [type of handgun]? You don't want us arming the teachers or having local residents open carrying to keep the school grounds safe. "Leave it to the cops," you say. But should the cops be going into a situation like that with nothing more than a layer of cotton uniform and a revolver to protect themselves and take down the bad guys? Or should they have to wait until a SWAT [special weapons and tactics] unit from an *appropriately large city* shows up, with the shooter mowing down third graders in the meantime?

While the shooting of Michael Brown *may* provide a teachable moment in terms of police interactions with the community, the nearly immediate mayhem that followed should also serve as a timely reminder. The old assumptions of law enforcement and their unwritten compact with the citizenry relied on a society where the police—and the laws—were respected, and criminals were a minority who would be rejected by the rank-and-file residents. But when the majority of an entire community decides to break that compact, the formula changes. They realize that they outnumber—and frequently outgun—the cops. A slumbering, snarling beast is awakened and in short order the police can find themselves on the run. This is not a formula for freedom of speech . . . it's the path to mayhem and the breakdown of civil society. Before you're too quick to demand the "demilitarization" of the police, you

---

1. In 1991, Rodney King, a black taxi driver, was beaten by Los Angeles police officers following a high-speed chase. When the officers involved were acquitted in 1992, massive riots began.
2. During the North Hollywood shootout, two heavily armed bank robbers engaged in heavy gunfire with Los Angeles police officers for a period of forty-four minutes.

might want to remember who it is that stands between the neighborhood you have now and South Central L.A. circa 1992. And Ferguson has shown us that you don't need a huge metropolitan area for it to happen.

Periodical and Internet Sources Bibliography

The following articles have been selected to supplement the diverse views presented in this chapter.

Sam Adler-Bell	"That's What You Get for Filming the Police," TruthOut, May 7, 2015.
Brian Beutler	"Police Unions Aren't the Problem," *New Republic*, May 7, 2015.
Sunil Dutta	"Hey Ferguson Protesters: Police Brutality Is Not the Problem," *Washington Post*, December 30, 2014.
Conor Friedersdorf	"Few Conservatives Take Police Abuses Seriously," *Atlantic*, May 1, 2015.
Dan Marcou	"6 Arguments Against the ACLU's Flawed 'Police Militarization' Report," PoliceOne.com, July 30, 2014.
Chris Mooney	"The Science of Why Cops Shoot Young Black Men," *Mother Jones*, December 2, 2014.
Jason L. Riley	"The Police Aren't the Problem," *Wall Street Journal*, December 10, 2014.
Mychal Denzel Smith	"Police Are the Problem," *Nation*, October 31, 2014.
Flint Taylor	"Darren Wilson Wasn't the First: A Short History of Killer Cops Let Off the Hook," *In These Times*, November 24, 2014.
D. Watkins	"Cops Are the Terrorists in Our Neighborhood: On Freddie Gray, Another Victim of Police Brutality," *Salon*, April 23, 2015.

CHAPTER 2

Is Police Brutality a Widespread Problem in the United States?

Chapter Preface

The incidents of police violence that took place across the United States in 2014 and 2015 generated a national conversation about the nature of America's law enforcement. Some claimed that the sheer amount of police brutality cases in so short a time indicated that the police believed themselves invincible, incapable of facing legal repercussions for using excessive force because their fellow officers would always protect them. Other commentators believed that reports of police brutality were isolated events involving abusive officers who in no way represented the rest of America's law enforcement.

Amid this ongoing discussion, famed former New York City police detective Frank Serpico wrote publicly that he is a member of the first group; police violence is systemic, he claimed, and almost no one is willing to do anything to change it. Serpico wrote from a position of experience, though in his own time, the issue had not been police brutality but corruption.

As a member of the New York City Police Department in the early 1970s, Serpico had staunchly refused to participate in the other officers' money-skimming plots, making him an outcast within his own department. His subsequent efforts to expose these officers and hold them legally responsible for their crimes were continually frustrated by the same kind of corruption at nearly every level of New York's legal bureaucracy. This also made Serpico's fellow officers truly hate him and even refuse to assist him on the job. One of the key factors in Serpico's decision to retire from the force in 1972 was a 1971 incident in which his backup police officers stood by while he was shot in the face by a suspect.

Writing about police brutality in *Politico* magazine in 2014, Serpico appealed to the same lessons he had learned more than forty years earlier: Violence takes place because police are only rarely held accountable for their actions, and no police department can ever successfully investigate itself because officers protect one another at every opportunity. According to Serpico, this creates a circular and nearly impenetrable problem, with police officers' perceived invulnerability making them more likely to perpetuate their excessively violent practices on the streets.

Serpico applied these accusations directly to the case in Ferguson, Missouri, where police officer Darren Wilson shot and killed criminal suspect Michael Brown in August 2014. Serpico questioned whether Wilson could have wounded Brown rather than kill him and criticized the way in which Wilson quickly garnered the support of police unions, which, Serpico asserted, usually partnered with district attorneys to secure legal protection for officers.

Serpico proposed several solutions to what he saw as systemic police brutality in the United States. These included stronger psychological screening of police recruits, better police training, mandatory community service for police officers, holding officers to the same legal standards as the rest of the American people, honoring honest and upstanding police, and creating independent civilian oversight committees to monitor police action. He noted that while some politicians were beginning to take some of these steps toward police reform, much more work still had to be done.

The following chapter presents various viewpoints that question the ubiquity of police brutality in America. Subjects discussed include the systemic nature of police violence, police brutality as a growing epidemic, and the effects of racism on police brutality.

> "The common assumption that police are generally using their authority in a trustworthy manner merits serious reconsideration."

Seven Reasons Police Brutality Is Systemic, Not Anecdotal

Bonnie Kristian

In the following viewpoint, Bonnie Kristian argues that brutality is widespread in America's police forces. As evidence that instances of unwarranted police violence are not simply anecdotal, she cites the militarization, inadequate training, and consistent racism of police departments across the United States. To Kristian, this constitutes a larger problem than only a few abusive officers. Kristian is a communications consultant for Young Americans for Liberty.

As you read, consider the following questions:

1. What does Kristian say produces inconsistent standards for judging the actions of police officers?

2. According to Kristian, how many of the ten thousand complaints filed against Chicago police between 2002 and 2004 resulted in disciplinary action?

3. What does Kristian say is the first step to preventing police brutality?

Darrin Manning's unprovoked "stop and frisk" encounter with the Philadelphia police left him hospitalized with a ruptured testicle. Neykeyia Parker was violently dragged out of her car and aggressively arrested in front of her young child for "trespassing" at her own apartment complex in Houston. A Georgia toddler was burned when police threw a flash grenade into his playpen during a raid, and the manager of a Chicago tanning salon was confronted by a raiding police officer bellowing that he would kill her and her family, captured on the salon's surveillance. An elderly man in Ohio was left in need of facial reconstructive surgery after police entered his home without a warrant to sort out a dispute about a trailer.

These stories are a small selection of recent police brutality reports, as police misconduct has become a fixture of the news cycle.

But the plural of anecdote is not data, and the media is inevitably drawn toward tales of conflict. Despite the increasing frequency with which we hear of misbehaving cops, many Americans maintain a default respect for the man in uniform. As an NYPD assistant chief put it, "We don't want a few bad apples or a few rogue cops damaging" the police's good name.

This is an attractive proposal, certainly, but unfortunately it doesn't hold up to scrutiny. Here are seven reasons why police misconduct is a systemic problem, not "a few bad apples":

1. Many departments don't provide adequate training in nonviolent solutions.

This is particularly obvious when it comes to dealing with family pets. "Police kill family dog" is practically its own subgenre of police brutality reports, and most of these cases—like

Community Grand Jury

GET OUT OF JAIL FREE

POLICE

POLICE MAY KEEP THIS CARD UNTIL NEEDED.

DARYL CAGLE POLITICALCARTOONS.COM   APOLOGIES TO HASBRO

© Daryl Cagle/Caglecartoons.com

the story of the Minnesota children who were made to sit, handcuffed, next to their dead and bleeding pet—are all too preventable. Some police departments have begun to train their officers to deal more appropriately with pets, but Thomas Aveni of the Police Policy Studies Council, a police consulting firm, says it's still extremely rare. In the absence of this training, police are less likely to view violence as a last resort.

2. Standards for what constitutes brutality vary widely.

"Excess is in the eyes of the beholder," explains William Terrill, a former police officer and professor of criminal justice at Michigan State. "To one officer 'objectively reasonable' means that if you don't give me your license, I get to use soft hands, and in another town the same resistance means I can pull you through the car window, [or] I can Tase you." The special deference police are widely given in American culture feeds this inconsistency of standards, producing something of a legal Wild West. While national legislation would likely only complicate matters further, local or statewide ballot propositions should allow the public—not the police—to define reasonable use of force.

3. Consequences for misconduct are minimal.

In central New Jersey, for instance, 99 percent of police brutality complaints are never investigated. Nor can that be explained away as stereotypical New Jersey corruption. Only one out of every three accused cops are convicted nationwide, while the conviction rate for civilians is literally double that. In Chicago, the numbers are even more skewed: There were 10,000 abuse complaints filed against the Chicago PD between 2002 and 2004, and just 19 of them "resulted in meaningful disciplinary action." On a national level, upwards of 95 percent of police misconduct cases referred for federal prosecution are declined by prosecutors because, as reported in *USA Today*, juries "are conditioned to believe cops, and victims' credibility is often challenged." Failure to remedy this police/civilian double standard cultivates an abuse-friendly legal environment.

4. Settlements are shifted to taxpayers.

Those officers who are found guilty of brutality typically find the settlement to their victims paid from city coffers. Research from Human Rights Watch reveals that in some places, taxpayers "are paying three times for officers who repeatedly commit abuses: once to cover their salaries while they commit abuses; next to pay settlements or civil jury awards against officers; and a third time through payments into police 'defense' funds provided by the cities." In larger cities, these settlements easily cost the public tens of millions of dollars annually while removing a substantial incentive against police misconduct.

5. Minorities are unfairly targeted.

"Simply put," says University of Florida law professor Katheryn K. Russell, "the public face of a police brutality victim is a young man who is black or Latino." In this case, research suggests perception matches reality. To give a particularly striking example, one Florida city's "stop and frisk" policy has been explicitly aimed at all black men. Since 2008, this has led to 99,980 stops that did *not* produce an arrest in a city with a population of just 110,000. One man alone was stopped 258 times at his job in four years, and arrested for trespassing while working on 62 occasions. Failure to address this issue communicates to police that minorities are a safe target for abuse.

6. Police are increasingly militarized.

During President Obama's gun control push, he argued that "weapons of war have no place on our streets;" but as Radley Balko has amply documented in his 2013 book, *Rise of the Warrior Cop*, local police are often equipped with weapons powerful enough to conquer a small country. Police use of highly armed SWAT teams has risen by 1,500 percent in the last two decades, and many police departments have cultivated an "us vs. them" mentality toward the public they ostensibly serve. Although possession of these weapons does not cause misconduct, as the old saying goes, when you have a hammer everything begins to look like a nail.

7. Police themselves say misconduct is remarkably widespread.

Here's the real clincher. A Department of Justice study revealed that a whopping 84 percent of police officers report that they've seen colleagues use excessive force on civilians, and 61 percent admit they don't always report "even serious criminal violations that involve abuse of authority by fellow officers."

This self-reporting moves us well beyond anecdote into the realm of data: Police brutality is a pervasive problem, exacerbated by systemic failures to curb it. That's not to say that every officer is ill-intentioned or abusive, but it is to suggest that the common assumption that police are generally using their authority in a trustworthy manner merits serious reconsideration. As John Adams wrote to [Thomas] Jefferson, "Power always thinks it has a great soul," and it cannot be trusted if left unchecked.

The good news is that the first step toward preventing police brutality is well-documented and fairly simple: Keep police constantly on camera. A 2012 study in Rialto, Calif., found that when officers were required to wear cameras recording all their interactions with citizens, "public complaints against officers plunged 88% compared with the previous 12 months. Officers' use of force fell by 60%." The simple knowledge that they were being watched dramatically altered police behavior.

Coupled with additional reforms, like making officers pay their own settlements and providing better training for dealing with pets, camera use could produce a significant decrease in police misconduct. It is not unrealistic to think that police brutality reports could be made far more unusual—but only once we acknowledge that it's *not* just a few bad apples.

| "*Some major recent police reforms got their start after highly publicized episodes of police violence.*"

History Indicates Varied Results in Improving Police Brutality in America

Nicole Flatow

In the following viewpoint, Nicole Flatow argues that recent American history has shown mixed results in improving police use of force. Episodes of police brutality involving victims Rodney King and Amadou Diallo, for example, led to some police reforms but did not do away with police violence entirely. Ultimately, Flatow believes, it often takes incidents of police brutality to implement reforms. Flatow is senior editor for ThinkProgress, a liberal blog.

As you read, consider the following questions:

1. What city does Flatow say originally militarized the police?

2. What does Flatow say was one of the most significant police reforms that emerged from Los Angeles's Christopher Commission?

3. Flatow says new legislation in New York City allows citizens to sue the police department for what offense?

A madou Diallo. Rodney King. Timothy Thomas. Looking at where we are today in the weeks after the shooting of Michael Brown in Ferguson, Missouri, it can feel like nothing has changed in the way we police the police.

Many things haven't. Juries acquitted police. Cops got their jobs back. And brutality happened again.

Some things have gotten worse. Like police militarization.

But some things have gotten better, or are still moving toward reform in the wake of a prominent brutality incident. A history of these incidents reveals that some major recent police reforms got their start after highly publicized episodes of police violence. But it was only after years or decades and dogged, persistent community building that some progress started to manifest.

Rodney King, 1991, Los Angeles

Videotape by a bystander captured five officers pummeling Rodney King with batons more than 50 times as he struggled on the ground outside his car. The recording immediately sparked outrage, but anger magnified when the officers who beat King were acquitted by a jury the following year. The acquittal triggered three days of violent riots during which at least 53 people died—and created immense momentum for reform. The cops in that case were ultimately held accountable when federal prosecutors took up the case and secured convictions of four officers. And by some measures, the LAPD [Los Angeles Police Department] was transformed in the two decades that followed.

Los Angeles was the original militarizer of police, even before the federal government started handing out leftover or used weapons and before the height of the war on drugs.

"The LAPD was the godfather of that kind of militaristic response," said John Jay College of Criminal Justice's Joe Domanick, author of a forthcoming book on LAPD reforms and the West Coast bureau chief for the Crime Report.

This is a very systemic problem in just about every community throughout the United States.

Los Angeles was forced to scale back in some ways after the riots, partially as a result of the Christopher Commission, created in response to the King beating to develop recommendations for reform. But initially, few of the commission's recommendations were adopted by the city.

"The Christopher Commission recommendations laid a foundation but weren't successful in bringing about reform," Domanick said.

One of the most significant reforms that did come out of the commission was ending the policy of lifetime terms for police chiefs. The police chief who presided during that period and had overseen an era of increased militarization at the Los Angeles Police Department, Daryl Gates, was forced to resign. And thereafter, lifetime terms were over.

But many things remained unresolved. For one thing, the mechanisms for policing the police didn't improve much. A Human Rights Watch report noted that "at risk" LAPD officers who frequently use significant force continued to act with impunity, and officers were not frequently punished for misbehavior, either internally or by the courts. For another, some tactics embraced by [New York City police commissioner Bill] Bratton have created their own set of hostilities with minority communities, as a result of policies that see targeting low-level offenses in high-crime areas as key to thwarting larger crime, Domanick said.

When this policy is not implemented with constant rigor, these police stops can also lead to unnecessary police violence and even death, as in the case of Ezell Ford, shot while reportedly laying on the ground after a routine police stop for still-undisclosed reasons.

Amadou Diallo, 1999, New York City

Plainclothes officers from the New York [City] Police Department shot street vendor Amadou Diallo just outside his Bronx apartment building after they mistook his wallet for a gun. These officers, too, were acquitted at trial.

Stop-and-frisk was actually getting worse, not better.

Then police commissioner Howard Safir instituted some changes after weeks of protest, including adding more minority officers to the special "Street Crimes" unit whose officer had shot Diallo and requiring all officers in the unit to wear uniforms.

But Darius Charney with the Center for Constitutional Rights [CCR] said these fixes were nothing more than cosmetic and lamented that the city initiated nothing like the Christopher Commission to reform itself. Weeks later, his organization honed in on what was perceived as the real issue uncovered by the shooting—the aggressive overuse of police stops. CCR filed a lawsuit to force reform, triggering a campaign against stop-and-frisk overuse in the NYPD that is still continuing.

At the time of the police shooting, the overwhelming police presence in some minority-heavy communities was a revelation to the general public. CCR's lawsuit sought data on the numbers and types of stops. For years, production of this data was delayed even after the city council passed a data collection law. But in 2006, outrage once again bubbled up when Sean Bell was killed by undercover cops in the wee morning hours of his wedding day, and the New York Civil Liberties Union compelled the city to release the data.

How the LA Riot Changed Police

Sunday [April 29, 2012] marks the 20th anniversary of the Los Angeles riot that followed the acquittal of four Los Angeles Police Department [LAPD] officers who were prosecuted by the state for using excessive force on Rodney King. There was extensive looting and burning, and 53 people lost their lives. . . .

The mainstream media failed miserably to explain why the Rodney King beating occurred. The increasing proliferation of video cameras guarantees that more and more police incidents will be captured. But the truth almost always lies deeper than the video.

How has the LAPD changed in 20 years? Ask a hundred people, and you'll likely get a hundred answers. . . .

- "Community policing" has taken hold in ways not seen in the past. The LAPD diversified to the point where Caucasian officers have been in the minority for many years. The city is on the verge of becoming majority Latino, and so is the department.

- The role of the civilian police commission (which had been the "boss" of the chief of police for many decades) was intensified, and an independent inspector general position was created.

- Use of force, whether minor or major, receives intense investigative scrutiny and command review. The Taser, pepper spray, and beanbag shotguns are used in greater numbers of incidents. . . .

- More than 2,000 additional officers were hired in an effort to achieve a (not-yet-realized) goal of 10,000.

Greg Meyer,
"How the Rodney King Riot Changed the LAPD,"
Police Magazine, *April 27, 2012.*

What this data revealed was that "stop-and-frisk was actually getting worse, not better," Charney said. The number of police stops had increased more than fivefold over the course of just five years, and they were just as racially skewed as they had ever been. With facts finally in hand, CCR filed a second lawsuit that resulted in a long-awaited victory when a federal judge held last year that the New York [City] Police Department had engaged in unconstitutional racial profiling.

Even now, the court has not yet enforced that order as the police unions hold up final resolution by attempting to intervene on the appeal that Mayor Bill de Blasio has already dropped. But using the momentum of that litigation, advocates were also able to successfully campaign for new city legislation to hold police accountable. One new bill creates an inspector general to oversee NYPD. Another allows citizens to sue the police department for profiling not just based on race but also sexual orientation, religion, housing status, and other discriminatory categories.

Timothy Thomas, 2001, Cincinnati

The big-city police departments in Los Angeles and New York have been under close watch both before and after these incidents, as they face the unique challenges and advantages of concentrated metropolitan areas. But perhaps an incident that most closely mirrors that in Ferguson is the 2001 shooting of Timothy Thomas by police that triggered riots in Cincinnati, Ohio. Thomas, a 19-year-old with an infant son, started to run when an officer approached him on the street outside a nightclub. The officer called in backup, a chase was on, and shots were fired with almost no information about Thomas. Cops said they thought Thomas was reaching for a gun but none was ever found.

The outcomes of the Cincinnati Collaborative Agreement were pretty astounding.

The officer in that case, too, was acquitted. But even before the verdict, community members responded to the shooting with intense riots and an economic boycott, exposing a history of racial tensions with police. Thomas was the 15th black man who died during a police confrontation in the six years before the riot. And by the time of Thomas's death, the perception was that Cincinnati faced intractable tensions between citizens and police that couldn't be fixed by yet another investigation or report. But public outrage along with federal intervention created the momentum for a different, expansive settlement in 2002 from litigation that started even before Thomas was killed. The pressure became so great that police stopped resisting and started collaborating.

As a result of agreements involving several advocacy groups and the Department of Justice, officers were trained on how to choose less-lethal force and how to deal with the mentally ill and those under the influence of drugs or alcohol. They even created a mental health response team. They were not just given Tasers, but also exhaustive training on when they could use them and how. If they used a Taser, they had to document their use. And if their record didn't match what was being reported, an investigation would ensue. Cars were equipped with dash cameras. They took "community policing seriously," doing walkthroughs of neighborhoods with residents, holding community meetings, and responding to community problems with nuanced solutions. Cincinatti's police chief has so embraced the reforms in the Collaborative Agreement that he takes a copy everywhere he goes.

And one more thing. Police were actually held accountable. Mike Brickner, senior policy director of the ACLU [American Civil Liberties Union] of Ohio, said one of the persistent problems the city encountered was that a few bad actors were committing egregious acts again and again without punishment and giving the entire department a bad name as a consequence. But after Thomas's death, a Citizen Police Review Board was formed that seemed to actually have buy-in from the police department. Officers were disciplined, given new training, or fired. Police and particularly police unions had resisted the accountability mechanisms "tooth and nail" for years before Thomas's death. But when public pressure became overwhelming, Brickner says even police unions fell in line. And in the end, many officers ended up liking the review mechanism, finding that it could be just as useful to exonerate an officer who had been wrongfully accused as to punish an officer for wrongdoing.

Post-Ferguson

The city of Ferguson will have its own local reforms to consider, as the council has already passed several bills to establish a police review board and set limits on excessive court fines and fees exposed after Brown's death. If past experience is any indication, reforming the police department is possible over the course of many years and many battles.

But nationally, problems persist. "This is a very systemic problem in just about every community throughout the United States," Brickner said.

The mentality is that these lives in the ghetto are not to be valued.

And even in communities that have seen dramatic change, there are as many holes left to be filled as there have been reforms. One is the intransigent, incredible challenge of holding police accountable. Police unions exercise strong influence over many local boards that decide whether cops get to keep their jobs. Juries tend to side with police. And the law overwhelmingly favors the police. UC [University of California] Irvine School of Law dean Erwin Chemerensky, who has long followed this issue, wrote after Brown's death that "the officer who shot Michael Brown and the city of Ferguson will most likely never be held accountable in court" due to doctrines from the Supreme Court that weigh against holding officers accountable.

Another is a culture that embraces guns. Police are given a lot of leeway to use deadly force, in many instances when the public perception is that other lesser measures might do. As CNN's Mark O'Mara noted after Brown's death, "Cops are doing the job we told them to do."

Riots in Ferguson have also exposed to America the extreme militarization of police forces that has only grown since the past waves of police shootings. And the racism in the criminal justice system persists, both overtly and implicitly, even as more whites than ever believe the criminal justice system is no longer biased.

In the case of Ferguson, U.S. attorney general Eric Holder has announced he will initiate an investigation of the city's "patterns and practices" in addition to the separate criminal investigation of the Brown case. In fact, Holder has taken on a new tone for the country's top law enforcer that acknowledges the United States' epidemic of discriminatory and overly punitive criminal punishment.

But underlying all of this is the segregation and oppression that was unveiled in Ferguson. A *Washington Post* investigation last week revealed that these underlying problems still persist in Cincinnati, meaning that while police were indeed reformed, fixing the racial tensions that existed in 2001 Cincinnati is "a job unfinished." Even Cincinnati's black police chief says he fears his own son's encounters with the police.

"The cultural disconnect is very real; you have the weight of generations of abuse on African Americans," Cincinnati police chief Jeffrey Blackwell told the *Washington Post* after Brown's death.

"[T]he mentality is that these lives in the ghetto are not to be valued," added Domanick. "Policing and violence are only symptoms of this larger problem. We're gonna have problems.

But at least we're starting to know now what works in terms of reducing crime short term and long term and what works in terms of community policing and good community relations."

86

> *"Expecting a cop to be held to the same
> level of accountability as your average,
> everyday citizen should not be much to
> ask for."*

Police Brutality Is a Growing American Epidemic

Colin Ochs

In the following viewpoint, Colin Ochs argues that police brutality is a widespread occurrence in the United States and is only getting worse. Bad cops are protected, Ochs says, by one another and by the court system, which perpetuates the problem. Ochs claims that police must be charged in court for violence, just as any other American citizen would be. Ochs is a writer for the Vanguard–Gainesville, the student newspaper of the University of North Georgia's Gainesville campus.

As you read, consider the following questions:

1. How many people does Ochs say were killed by police in 2014?

2. According to Ochs, how did Officer Grant Morrison justify his killing of Richard Ramirez in Billings, Montana?

3. Who does Ochs blame for allowing police to form the attitude that they can get away with anything?

W e've all heard about Eric Garner [an unarmed black man killed by police in Staten Island, New York] and Michael Brown [unarmed, eighteen-year-old black man killed by a police officer in Ferguson, Missouri]. You've also probably heard of Tamir Rice [twelve-year-old black boy brandishing a toy gun who was shot by police in Cleveland, Ohio] and John Crawford [a black man carrying an air rifle through a Walmart near Dayton, Ohio, who was shot by police].

If you think these are the only instances where a cop has killed an unarmed civilian, then you are gravely mistaken. This is an epidemic we have on our hands. If citizens aren't being killed by the police, they are being unlawfully harassed and mistreated with no consequence to the officer.

The time for this to stop is now.

Different Standards

Before I go any further, I should emphasize that I know not all cops are cruel. In fact, the majority of them are probably good. This [viewpoint] focuses on getting rid of the abusive cops and holding them accountable for their actions.

I will not be focusing on the previously mentioned cases, since I'm sure you have already formed opinions about those.

It's hard to pick just a couple of cases to talk about, however, because 1,103 people have been killed by police in 2014 alone. This is according to multiple citizen-run databases such as Killed by Police on Facebook. The man who runs this page documents every person killed by police and numbers them next to their news bulletin. So far, he's gathered 1,944 police killings since May 1, 2013.

Not all of these police killings are unjustified, but help me justify the case of 38-year-old Richard Ramirez.

Ramirez was gunned down in his car by Officer Grant Morrison during a traffic stop in Billings, Montana, in April 2014. According to the website thefreethoughtproject.com, all the justification Morrison needed to kill an unarmed Ramirez and get away scot-free was to claim that he saw Ramirez "reach for his waistband."

I thought police officers were supposed to be brave. Even if Ramirez did, in fact, reach for his waistband—and there is a strong possibility that he didn't, as officers have been caught lying on the stand before, like when five Chicago officers got caught lying about a case as reported by the *Chicago Tribune*, you better be absolutely sure that there is a gun before you shoot.

If it is proven that the man you shot was unarmed, you should face the same charges that every other citizen would face. I don't believe anyone would be convicted of murder, or at the very least manslaughter, if the only defense needed was "I saw him reach for his waistband."

How about the case of 29-year-old United States Army veteran Denis Reynoso?

Reynoso was gunned down in his own home in Lynn, Massachusetts, on Sept. 5, 2013, after cops entered his house without a warrant in response to a noise complaint. That's right, a simple noise complaint. It was discovered that he was murdered in front of his 5-year-old son, no less, when the child was found covered in his daddy's blood after Jessica Spinney, Reynoso's fiancée, arrived at the scene.

After Reynoso was shot three times, the cops tore his house apart looking for drugs or weapons. They, of course, found nothing.

Lynn Police are trying to justify the murder by claiming that Reynoso had grabbed an officer's gun, resulting in them gunning him down. The *Bay State Examiner* wrote a very thorough investigative article about the incident in which it shows video interviews of the three officers involved contradicting each other's stories during the investigation of the event. The district attorney's office never asked the officers about their contradictory statements.

There is an obvious conflict of interest whenever a district attorney's office conducts an investigation involving a police force that works with them. District attorneys (DAs) use police department investigations to solve crimes. If the credibility of the police departments in a DA's district comes into question, it could put other cases at risk.

A Sweeping Epidemic

There is a reason police have been cleared of every single one of the 73 fatal police shootings in Massachusetts since 2002.

Police will never be held accountable as long as their district attorneys are conducting the investigations. It's not that hard to get an independent third party to conduct these investigations, but a DA's office is not going to do that voluntarily in fear of what it might do [to] their jobs.

This whole system of everyone trying to cover their own lies, with no one questioning them or being allowed to question them, is leaving bad cops who feel like they can get away with anything on the streets. And why wouldn't they feel that way? We, as a society, are setting a dangerous precedent that cops can get away with anything.

There are too many cases of children having to grow up without one or both of their parents, spouses being thrust into raising a child on their own, and parents being forced to bury their children because cops are being allowed to kill without fear of repercussion.

This will not go away unless we stand up for those who cannot stand anymore.

Police killings are happening all over the country at an alarming rate. An average of three people a day were killed by

Police Brutality Is an Epidemic

Recent news coverage of high-profile shootings ... have arguably raised public awareness of the fact that police abuse is a problem, but without data, it is hard to make a strong case regarding what to do about the perpetuation of overpolicing and police abuse throughout the country.

Facts don't lie. The more the public is armed with facts, the better advocates can make the case for systemic overhauls. . . .

- The number of people killed by police in 2014: 1,149, according to Mapping Police Violence, a research collaborative collecting data on police killings nationwide.

- The number of people killed by police so far in 2015: 470, according to the *Guardian*.

- The percentage of those people who were women: 4.6%, or 22 people, according to the *Guardian*.

- Of those women, the percentage who were women of color: roughly 41%, or 9 people, according to the *Guardian*. . . .

- The likelihood that a black person killed by police, like 22-year-old Rekia Boyd (killed in Chicago), will be unarmed: Twice as likely as a white person killed by police, according to the *Guardian*.

- The group as likely as black Americans to be killed by police, according to 1999–2013 data from the Centers for Disease Control and Prevention: Native Americans. . . .

- The number of centralized and federally operated up-to-date police misconduct tracking systems: Zero.

Darnell L. Moore, "25 Shocking Facts About the Epidemic of Police Brutality in America," Mic.com, June 3, 2015.

cops last year [2014] and 72 have already been killed in a year. That was only 25 days old at the time of this writing, and may have risen since (see: Killed by Police Facebook page).

Here in Georgia, according to the First Coast News, Jack Lamar Roberson was killed by police after his parents called 911 asking for medical help for their son, who they feared was contemplating suicide. Cops came in and shot him without saying a word.

It's a shame that I can't talk about every unarmed citizen killed by cops in this [viewpoint], which would take a *Lord of the Rings*–sized novel to do. I urge all of you to check out thefreethoughtproject.com and innocentdown.org as well as follow Cop Block and Killed by Police on Facebook to really understand the full scope of this problem.

Again, I reiterate that the majority of cops are good and serve our community in a way that deserves our respect, but as the saying goes, "a chain is only as strong as its weakest link." Well, in my opinion, there are a lot of weak links out there "protecting our freedom."

These cops view society as a war zone, and we are the enemy. Don't remain silent just because this issue hasn't personally affected you yet.

Speak up now! Demand justice for those who have fallen. Expecting a cop to be held to the same level of accountability as your average, everyday citizen should not be much to ask for. I don't want there to be a war on cops, but that's the road we're headed for if things don't change.

| "Only in the fevered imagination of the
cop-hating ideologue is 'police brutality'
a national crisis, or any sort of crisis."

Police Brutality Is Not a Growing Epidemic

Jack Kerwick

In the following viewpoint, Jack Kerwick argues that police brutality is not an epidemic in the United States. To prove this, he notes statistics showing that extremely small percentages of Americans have actually experienced force by police. Conversely, he claims, large percentages of people have reported that they were satisfied with police responses to their requests for help. Kerwick is a writer for FrontPage Magazine, *an online journal of news and political commentary.*

As you read, consider the following questions:

1. What does Kerwick say is wrong with the phrase "police brutality"?

2. According to Kerwick, what percentage of the forty-four million Americans who interacted with police in 1999 were threatened with or experienced force?

3. What two ethnic groups does Kerwick say have been most satisfied with police responses to their situations?

Recently, I claimed that everyone—politicians, academics, and media commentators—who promoted the idea that police brutality is a national "epidemic," or even a "growing concern," as one self-styled libertarian put it, share some culpability for the murders of the two NYPD [New York City Police Department] officers who were gunned down in their vehicle right before Christmas [in 2014].

More specifically, they are responsible, obviously, not for intending or consciously encouraging the murder of police, but for creating a climate for police officers that's even more hostile than that in which officers must spend their days and nights. After all, we don't need Richard Weaver [a conservative scholar] to inform us that "ideas have consequences." Even simpletons and liars will concede this much.

And only simpletons and liars can deny that this idea—the idea of a "pandemic" of police brutality sweeping the nation—has the consequence of endangering police officers.

Yet this idea isn't just dangerous.

It is also a lie. And it is a huge lie at that.

The Epidemic Lie

"Police brutality" is an all-purpose piece of rhetoric that, as such, can mean anything and everything—and, thus, nothing at all. When anti-police misologists—a "misologist" was the word that the 18th-century philosopher Immanuel Kant used when referring to an enemy of reason—sound off about "police brutality," they are referring to the police's unjustified use of force.

Now, all but anarchists concede that police are authorized to use force when necessary and when it's proportionate to the situation in question. When, however, the force deployed

Reporting Incidents on the Rise

One expert says that America is suffering from a misperception: There really isn't any increase in police brutality, only an increase in the reporting of incidents due to a proliferation of cell phones and portable video devices in the hands of the populace.

In an August 12 [2012] article at the *Wall Street Journal*, Maria Haberfeld, a professor at John Jay College of Criminal Justice in New York, insisted that there is no real growth in police brutality.

Despite the story in Ferguson, Missouri [where a police officer shot and killed Michael Brown], or that of the New York man [Eric Garner] who died from a choke hold delivered by police there, Haberfeld says it is a misperception that police are increasingly resorting to violence. . . .

Concerning how use of force is judged, Haberfeld insisted, "To an untrained eye, somebody that doesn't understand police work, it may look skewed towards law enforcement, but it's really not."

She went on to say, "We have to remember that we have over half a million armed police officers in this country. If police officers were really so trigger happy . . . we would have many more bodies on a daily basis than we have. It's really very rare to see a police encounter in which someone ends up dead."

Warner Todd Houston, "Expert: No Rise in Use of Deadly Force by Police; Just More Cell Phones," Breitbart, August 13, 2014.

is unnecessary and/or excessive, then the force is unjustified. This—the unnecessary and/or excessive use of force—is "police brutality."

So, is this a growing national phenomenon, an epidemic? Not even close.

According to the Department of Justice's Office of Community Oriented Policing Services (COPS), in 1999, of 44 million people who had face-to-face interactions with police officers, less than one-half of one percent was "threatened with or actually experienced force."

Notice, the assertion here isn't that less than one-half of one percent—it bears repeating: one-half of one percent—was subjected to the use of unjustified force; the claim is that of 44 million, this miniscule fraction of people were either threatened with—threatened with—or subjected to the use of force per se.

What this in turn means is that the number of people who were "brutalized" by police is even smaller than "less than one-half of one percent."

According to the Bureau of Justice Statistics' Police-Public Contact Survey (PPCS), of a national population estimate of roughly 240,000,000 comprised of people of 16 years of age or older, of those who dealt with the police in some capacity in 2002, 2005, and 2008, 1.5%, 1.6%, and 1.4%, respectively, were either threatened with or subjected to force by the police.

In 2008, 22% of those falling into the latter group admitted that they "argued with, cursed at, insulted, or verbally threatened the police." Twelve percent reported that they were "disobeying" and/or "interfering" with police.

Of the 84% of people who felt that the threat or use of police force was "improper," only 14% filed a complaint.

To further underscore just what a whopper of a lie is the notion that "police brutality" is a nationwide epidemic, consider this: Among those included in the class of people who have had to deal with police are those who have called on the police for assistance. And among those who have done so, about 85 percent claimed to have been "satisfied with the police response." Moreover—shocker of shockers!—Hispanics (86%) and blacks (85%) were slightly more satisfied than were whites (83%). Finally, about 90 percent of people who requested police assistance said that they would do so again.

Only in the fevered imagination of the cop-hating ideologue is "police brutality" a national crisis, or any sort of crisis.

The Nonsense Dogma

Of course, none of this is to deny that there are bad cops. Genuinely abusive police officers, like those who abuse their power and authority anywhere, deserve to be crucified. But there is zero justification for abstracting from these relatively few instances a rule encompassing police officers generally.

Numbers aside, just some rudimentary common sense—a rare commodity nowadays, and practically nonexistent among the police-hating ideologues—should determine that in this Age of the Camera—a time in which everyone and their mother is armed with surveillance apparatus—the police have no real option but to be better behaved than ever before.

[British philosopher] Jeremy Bentham described the doctrine of "natural rights" as "nonsense on stilts." The dogma—and make no mistakes about it, for the anti-police misologists, this is nothing less than a dogma—that "police brutality" is an epidemic, a crisis, blah, blah, blah, is indeed nonsense on stilts. But it is more than this: It is nonsense that kills.

> *"There is a remarkable dearth of out-rage from white Americans when their countrymen of color are denied the most fundamental right—life—by the police."*

White America's Silence on Police Brutality Is Consent

Donovan X. Ramsey

In the following viewpoint, Donovan X. Ramsey argues that white Americans should more forcefully protest the treatment of African Americans by police. Minorities, Ramsey says, are disproportionately targeted for police violence and need the help of outraged white Americans to escape this. White silence on this issue, he concludes, will perpetuate the disenfranchisement of African Americans. Ramsey is a contributing journalist for numerous news outlets and is also a Demos Emerging Voices fellow.

As you read, consider the following questions:

1. According to Ramsey, what was the percentage increase of white Americans' understanding of police racism between 1969 and 2014?

2. According to Ramsey, why is police reform directly related to white Americans' responding appropriately to abuse by police?

3. According to Ramsey's source, why do white Americans remain silent on the issue of police brutality against African Americans?

Late Tuesday, news broke that yet another unarmed American, a black man named Walter Scott, was killed by a white police officer. As with Tamir Rice, Eric Garner, and Rodney King nearly 25 years ago, the brutality was captured on video for the world to see. The *New York Times* put the damning evidence at the very top of its homepage, and it quickly spread throughout social media networks, provoking outrage, disgust, horror, grief. These reactions have come most vocally from black Americans. The silence from white activists, elected officials, public figures, and citizens has been deafening.

If you're white and have made it to this paragraph you might be thinking, or headed to the comments to write, "not all white people . . ." To be sure, there are white Americans active in efforts toward police reform. That population is, however, nowhere near the critical mass needed for change. Take for example New York City mayor Bill de Blasio. He made some unprecedented comments expressing "pain and frustration" after a grand jury failed to indict the NYPD officer who choked Eric Garner to death on film. He was quickly pressured to walk back that sentiment and, without the support he needed, did exactly that.

The bottom line: The majority of white Americans believe the nation's police are doing a good job despite that work often ending in the deaths of unarmed black people.

In every major speech on race that President Obama has delivered during his presidency, he has reassured Americans of our collective will to form a more perfect union. When his

2008 campaign was in danger of being derailed by his Chicago pastor, Obama remarked on the "vast majority" of Americans who want a more equitable country. After George Zimmerman was acquitted of murder charges for killing Trayvon Martin, Obama reminded us that, "Each successive generation seems to be making progress in changing attitudes when it comes to race." And, when a grand jury failed to indict a white officer for choking a black Staten Island man to death, the president instructed: ". . . it is incumbent upon all of us, as Americans, regardless of race, region, faith, that we recognize this is an American problem."

Black Americans are largely on board with making police brutality an issue of urgent national interest. We've always been desperate for change. White Americans, not so much.

According to Harris polls, white Americans have been slow to accept that racism plays a harmful role in policing. Between 1969 and 2014, white Americans' understanding that blacks are generally discriminated against by the police has only increased from 19 percent in 1969 to a paltry 48 percent in 2014. Progress, but still short of a majority. Meanwhile, black endorsement of that statement has stayed relatively stable, increasing just 10 points from 76 percent to 86 percent during the same period.

When we can't complete a news cycle without learning another unarmed black person has been killed by police, one wonders: Where are the reasonable white Americans? Where's the religious right, those patriots and lovers of life and liberty? Even more, where are those good white cops, and what do they have to say about the one who executed Scott and then had the clarity of mind to possibly plant a weapon near him and falsify a police report?

There is a remarkable dearth of outrage from white Americans when their countrymen of color are denied the most fundamental right—life—by the police. City-level polling data from Los Angeles and New York reveals that white approval of the police is consistently high in those cities—despite the checkered history of their police departments. It drops on average somewhere around 10 points when there are high-profile cases of police brutality but, irrespective of what remedies follow, it recovers to pre-incident levels in no time.

And make no mistake about it, police reform in this country is dependent on white Americans taking incidents of abuse seriously. White people are the nation's largest and most empowered racial voting bloc, and their perception of crime, fairness, and justice is perhaps one of the most influential factors in law enforcement. Public sentiment aside, white Americans make up—the vast majority—nearly 80 percent—of this nation's police force.

So, what do they think? Well, it seems we have a system of policing—brutality included—that the vast majority of white Americans approve of, or, at the very least, tolerate.

Whites rate the nation's police force among the three institutions in our country that inspire the most confidence, behind only the military and small business, according to a survey by Gallup. In fact, white Americans admire the police more than they do clergy. With that in mind, it should be no surprise then that 70 percent of white Americans say they can imagine a situation in which they would approve of a police officer striking a citizen. Nearly the same share approve of police hitting suspects trying to escape from custody.

Sixty percent of white Americans surveyed by ABC News in December said that the killings of Michael Brown in Ferguson and Garner in New York City were isolated incidents. Robin DiAngelo is a professor of multicultural education at Westfield State University and the author of *What Does It Mean to Be White?* In her work on white silence in racial discussions, DiAngelo explains that such reduction of systematic racism to a series of similar but isolated events aids white silence. She writes, "much of the rationale for white silence is based on a racial paradigm that posits racism as isolated to

Police Union at War with City Officials

Pittsburgh's new police chief has been criticized by a police union president for being photographed on New Year's Eve holding a sign that says: 'I resolve to challenge racism @ work.'

The sign also has a Twitter hashtag that says '# end white silence.' Chief Cameron McLay was photographed holding up the sign that someone had brought to the city's annual First Night celebration.

Mayor Bill Peduto said he saw the picture on social media and liked it so much he reposted it on his own Facebook page.

"I thought, 'What a great way to begin the new year,'" said the first-year mayor, who hired McLay in September [2014].

Peduto said he believes the chief was simply recognizing that racism exists and acknowledging there's work to be done restoring trust between the city's police and the black community.

But Fraternal Order of Police president Howard McQuillan said the sign paints city police as racists and violates a policy governing police participation in social media. McQuillan took issue with the mayor's previous comments criticizing the police and saying departmental reforms were needed. . . .

"By Mayor Peduto labeling us 'corrupt and mediocre' and now our current chief insinuating that we are now racist, merely by the color of our skin and the nature of our profession, I say enough is enough!" [McQuillan] said.

Associated Press, "Cops at War over Photo of Pittsburgh Police Chief with Sign Demanding an End to 'White Silence' with a Pledge to 'Challenge Racism at Work,'" Daily Mail, January 4, 2015.

individual acts of meanness that only some people do. This dominant paradigm of racism as discrete, individual, intentional, and malicious acts makes it unlikely that whites will see our silence as a function of, and support to, racism and white privilege." White silence around race, as a result, functions to maintain white supremacy and ultimately harms people of color, she argues.

That brings us back to an unarmed Scott, stopped for a busted taillight in a state where you're only required to have one, struck five times from behind as he ran away from a man who'd later appeared to plant evidence on his dead body and lie about administering CPR to him. And, of course, Scott brings us back to Miriam Carey, Aiyana Stanley-Jones, Ezell Ford, John Crawford, and so many others. How many more must die, how close together, and under what circumstances before the most empowered Americans feel compelled to advance, legislate and execute police reform? Or is this the system they want?

Is Police Brutality a Widespread Problem in the United States?

VIEWPOINT

6

> "*The driving force behind the eruption of police violence in the United States is class oppression.*"

Police Brutality in America Is About Class, Not Race

Joseph Kishore

In the following viewpoint, Joseph Kishore argues that police brutality in the United States does not result from racism but rather from class warfare. Police target minorities for violence, he believes, not specifically because of their race but because they are members of the lowest economic class in the country. According to Kishore, this perpetuates the rule of the statist American aristocracy while keeping the working class weak and disenfranchised. Kishore is a writer for the World Socialist Web Site.

As you read, consider the following questions:

1. According to Kishore, how have the deaths of African Americans at the hands of police provided an opportunity for the state to build up the apparatus of repression in America?

2. What does Kishore say is wrong with President Obama's response to police violence?

3. What does Kishore say the United States is expressing with the building up of its police state?

Four months ago today, Michael Brown, an unarmed teenager, was shot and killed by a police officer in Ferguson, Missouri [in August 2014]. Popular anger over yet another police murder in the United States has only deepened in the weeks and months since, fueled by the decisions of highly manipulated grand juries not to charge the police officer who killed Brown or the police officer who choked to death Eric Garner in Staten Island last July.

The response of the ruling class to these events has run along two interconnected channels. On the one hand, the protests have been utilized as an opportunity to build up the apparatus of repression even further, including the declaration of a preemptive state of emergency in Ferguson last month and the deployment of the National Guard against protests.

At the same time, the ruling elite is mobilizing the practitioners of identity politics, whose job is to insist that the killing of Brown and Garner, and the exoneration of the police officers who killed them, are entirely the result of racism. The aim is to obscure the fundamental class issues involved and maintain the political authority of the very state apparatus that is responsible for repression and violence throughout the country.

The Pervading Opinion

[President Barack] Obama himself took the lead in an interview aired yesterday on Black Entertainment Television. Feigning sympathy for the protesters, Obama urged "patience" and "persistence." Racism, he said, "is deeply rooted in our society, it's deeply rooted in our history."

Seeking to leverage the fact that he is the country's first African American president, Obama said that the issue "is not only personal for me, because of who I am and who Michelle is and who our family members are and what our experiences are, but as president, I consider this to be one of the most important issues we face." He added, "America works when everybody feels as if they are being treated fairly."

Obama added that the outcome of the Garner case, in particular, "gives us the opportunity to have the conversation [on race] that has been a long way coming."

As always, the president's comments were shot through with hypocrisy and deceit. The homilies about everyone being "treated fairly" were delivered by a president who has made sure that no punishment was meted out to the financial swindlers who caused the Wall Street crash or the CIA [Central Intelligence Agency] and [George W.] Bush administration officials who oversaw and carried out torture.

As for the pretense of concern over police brutality, Obama made his position absolutely clear last week when the White House announced there would be no letup in the programs that funnel billions of dollars in military equipment to local police forces throughout the country.

In presenting himself as a supporter of those protesting police violence, Obama seeks to exploit his racial background, an effort that is buttressed by a network of lavishly paid political scoundrels such as Al Sharpton, the multimillionaire former FBI [Federal Bureau of Investigation] informant who invariably anoints himself the leader of every protest against police brutality. After meeting with the president last week, Sharpton called for a march in Washington next weekend aimed at directing popular anger over police violence into the harmless channel of appeals to Congress and the Obama administration.

These maneuvers have been accompanied by a series of articles in the "left" media insisting that the fundamental issue in the killing of Garner and Brown is "white supremacy" (in the words of one *Rolling Stone* article), "white privilege" and racial oppression.

One of the foulest pieces was penned by Rutgers University professor Brittney Cooper and published on Salon.com. In "White America's scary delusion: Why its sense of black humanity is so skewed," Cooper denounces the "ignorance and lack of empathy" of "white folks," who benefit from "the violence at the core of the ideology of whiteness."

From the International Socialist Organization [ISO], the basic line is the same. In "When racism wears a badge," the ISO's Keeanga-Yamahtta Taylor writes of the "terrorism that pervades black and brown communities," and of a racist system that has "criminalized and impoverished African Americans." While Taylor refers to "black" and "African American" more than 30 times, the word "class" does not appear. As for Obama, he is mentioned only to criticize him for not sufficiently focusing on questions of race.

Real Class Conflict

These people have an agenda. It is to encourage divisions along racial lines within the working class. According to them, the basic problem is not capitalism, a system based on class exploitation and oppression, of which racial discrimination is one expression, but rather a hatred of blacks that is somehow built into the genetic code of white people. On this basis it is a natural and inevitable progression to support black Democrats and their bourgeois allies and oppose an independent and united movement of the working class against the entire political establishment.

This is not to deny the existence of racism, which is encouraged among the more backward layers recruited into the police. Yet the violence directed at Brown, Garner and countless other workers and youth is far more about socioeconomic class than about race. While African Americans are dispropor-

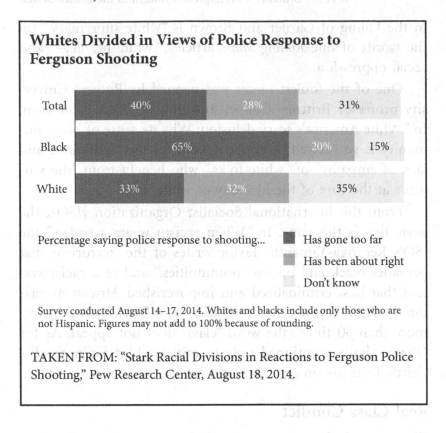

Whites Divided in Views of Police Response to Ferguson Shooting

	Has gone too far	Has been about right	Don't know
Total	40%	28%	31%
Black	65%	20%	15%
White	33%	32%	35%

Percentage saying police response to shooting...
■ Has gone too far
■ Has been about right
■ Don't know

Survey conducted August 14–17, 2014. Whites and blacks include only those who are not Hispanic. Figures may not add to 100% because of rounding.

TAKEN FROM: "Stark Racial Divisions in Reactions to Ferguson Police Shooting," Pew Research Center, August 18, 2014.

tionately the targets of police killings, white workers and youth still comprise the majority of victims. It is often black police commissioners and black mayors—and even black presidents—who oversee the oppression of minority youth.

The insistence, bordering on hysteria, with which political forces around the Democratic Party proclaim race to be the fundamental social category in America is proportional to the degree this brand of politics is being discredited—particularly by the experience of the Obama administration itself.

Obama, promoted by the likes of the *Nation* and the ISO as the "transformative candidate" six years ago, has presided over a historic reversal in the living conditions of workers of all races. Well into the Obama administration's supposed "recovery," social inequality in the United States is higher than at any point since the Great Depression of the 1930s, thanks to the massive transfer of wealth to Wall Street it has engineered.

Social polarization has grown the most among African Americans and other ethnic minorities, with the great majority suffering a decline in living standards and a small elite growing wealthy from programs such as affirmative action and their incorporation into the political and corporate establishment. Obama is, in fact, the embodiment of this corrupt and reactionary social layer.

In Detroit, which is overwhelmingly African American, an African American emergency manager, working closely with the Obama administration, has overseen the plundering of the city in the interests of the financial aristocracy, including huge cuts in the pensions and health benefits of active and retired city workers. Wages for the working class as a whole, and particularly industrial workers, have plummeted. Public schools and social infrastructure have been relentlessly attacked.

All of this has an impact on popular consciousness, encouraging the understanding that it is class, not race, which determines government policy. The identity politics that has become a mainstay of bourgeois rule in the United States over the past four decades has suffered a severe blow. The likes of Jesse Jackson [African American civil rights activist, minister, and politician] and Al Sharpton, and the milieu of political organizations rooted in identity politics and based on affluent layers of the upper-middle class, are themselves increasingly despised.

The driving force behind the eruption of police violence in the United States is class oppression. The combination of imperialist war abroad and social counterrevolution at home is expressed politically in the erection of a police state apparatus directed ever more openly against social and political opposition within the United States.

The conflict between the financial aristocracy and the working class is the fundamental source of the brutality and violence of the state. The same conflict creates the objective foundation for a political movement that can put an end to this brutality: an independent and united movement of the entire working class, in opposition to capitalism and all of its political defenders.

Periodical and Internet Sources Bibliography

The following articles have been selected to supplement the diverse views presented in this chapter.

Lulu Chang	"Do Police Shoot Black Men More Often? Statistics Say Yes, Absolutely," Bustle, August 18, 2014.
Colleen Curry	"Police Unions' Defense of 'Bad Cops' Draws Criticism in Brutality Debate," Vice News, May 5, 2015.
Conor Friedersdorf	"The Brutality of Police Culture in Baltimore," *Atlantic*, April 22, 2015.
Braden Goyette, Nick Wing, and Danielle Cadet	"21 Numbers That Will Help You Understand Why Ferguson Is About More than Michael Brown," *Huffington Post*, August 22, 2014.
Joseph Kishore	"Capitalism, the Working Class and the Fight Against Police Violence," World Socialist Web Site, May 1, 2015.
Dana Liebelson and Ryan J. Reilly	"Feds Find Shocking, Systemic Brutality, Incompetence in Cleveland Police Department," *Huffington Post*, December 5, 2014.
Darnell L. Moore	"25 Shocking Facts About the Epidemic of Police Brutality in America," Mic.com, June 3, 2015.
Mark Robison	"Fact Checker: Is Police Brutality Toward Blacks Rare?," *Reno Gazette-Journal*, August 25, 2014.
Frank Serpico	"The Police Are Still Out of Control," *Politico*, October 23, 2014.
Paul Joseph Watson	"Black Crime Facts That the White Liberal Media Daren't Talk About," Infowars.com, May 5, 2015.

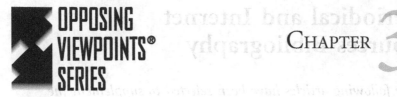

OPPOSING
VIEWPOINTS®
SERIES

CHAPTER 3

How Can Police Brutality Be Stopped?

Chapter Preface

In 2014 and 2015, the cities of Ferguson, Missouri; New York, New York; and Baltimore, Maryland, garnered national attention for the incidents of apparent police brutality that occurred there. In all of these cases, the actions of white police officers led to the deaths of African Americans that the black community labeled as wrongful and unnecessary. These tragedies had been allowed to happen, objectors claimed, because of the institutionalized aggression and racism of America's police. The deaths quickly ignited major riots in these and other cities around the United States, with activists calling for police accountability and justice for these deaths.

Protests became especially heated in New York in December 2014, when a grand jury decided not to indict a police officer whose alleged choke hold had killed forty-three-year-old Eric Garner the previous July. Police had been attempting to arrest Garner for selling untaxed cigarettes, but he ultimately died during the incident. In December, the grand jury's decision generated large-scale protests in many locations throughout New York City. Protestors labeled the police as terrorists and Ku Klux Klan members, referring to the white supremacy organization that at one time harassed and murdered African Americans. Garner's last words before his death, "I can't breathe," quickly became a slogan meant to emphasize the helplessness of the people at the hands of what they saw as the abusive and authoritarian police force.

Weeks later, a gunman shot two New York City police officers to death in their patrol car before killing himself. He had previously written on social media that his actions were vengeance against the police for the death of Eric Garner. Amid the tense atmosphere in the city that month, New York mayor Bill de Blasio generated his own controversy when he appeared to sympathize with protestors accusing the police of racism and brutality. This greatly angered city police officers, who accused de Blasio of stoking civilian animosity toward them.

As a result, the New York City Police Department (NYPD) organized its own form of public protest against de Blasio. When the mayor entered a Brooklyn hospital to visit the bodies of the two murdered officers, the attending police officers silently turned their backs to him. Police repeated this gesture again when de Blasio spoke at the graduation of NYPD recruits. Finally, at the funerals of the two officers, one held in late December 2014 and the other in early January 2015, the thousands of police in attendance again turned away from de Blasio as he eulogized the deceased.

De Blasio later angrily expressed to the media that police officers protesting at the funerals had acted highly inappropriately. The mayor's critics, including New York police union leader Patrick Lynch, attested that the officers deserved to protest in any manner they chose because de Blasio, through his comments, had intensified the city's hostility toward police. This, in Lynch's view, even made de Blasio responsible for the deaths of the two officers. Events such as these in New York began a nationwide discussion of the proper settings in which to protest police actions, with some arguing for the American people's right to do so at any time and others asserting that police deserve to be honored, not vilified, for their dedication to protecting and serving.

The following chapter presents viewpoints on various proposed methods of stopping police brutality. Topics include police body cameras, protests against police, and civilian oversight of police activity.

> *"Having a video record of events not only deters the use of excessive force, but it also helps dispute or demonstrate claims of police brutality."*

Body Cameras Will Stop Police Brutality

Adam Schiff

In the following viewpoint, Adam Schiff argues for the benefits of requiring American police officers to wear body cameras. This would not only deter police brutality, he writes, but also would create clear records of police activity that could be referred to later. Schiff is the Democratic US congressman from California's twenty-eighth district.

As you read, consider the following questions:

1. According to Schiff, in what way does Rialto, California, provide an example of the benefits of police body cameras?

2. What does Schiff say is the problem many police departments experience when considering implementing body cameras?

Adam Schiff, "Crescenta Valley Weekly Op-Ed: Department of Justice Should Play a Role in Funding Body Cameras for Local Police Departments," Congressman Adam Schiff, September 25, 2014. Courtesy of Congressman Adam Schiff.

3. What options does Schiff suggest to help police departments pay for body cameras?

The sights and sounds we witnessed in Ferguson, Missouri, during the protests following the death of Michael Brown are hard to forget—violent out-of-town agitators disrupting peaceful protests, tear gas, rocks and gunshots, police on the streets in full riot and military gear, and vehicles that look more suited to Iraq than a suburb of St. Louis. The shooting of an unarmed African American youth exposed deep racial divides and the endemic mistrust between many minority communities and the police departments that serve them.

As the investigation into the death of Michael Brown illustrates, the circumstances of an officer-involved shooting can arouse the strongest passions in a community and breed an atmosphere of profound distrust. It doesn't have to be this way. By encouraging models of policing that engage with the community and neighborhoods in a constructive and non-confrontational way, both police and civilians are better served. One such approach would make use of a relatively new technology: small, lightweight body cameras.

Positive Returns

Cities around the country have started to adopt cameras for their officers to create a record of police interactions, and the early returns are positive. Having a video record of events not only deters the use of excessive force, but it also helps dispute or demonstrate claims of police brutality. And in either case, it improves community confidence in a just result. Studies done in localities that have implemented body-worn cameras have shown a positive impact by demonstrating a commitment to transparency and accountability and helping to de-escalate potentially tense interactions.

A study conducted of the Rialto, California, police department from 2012 to 2013 showed the potential of cameras.

Police Use of Body Cameras Is Expanding

"On-officer recording systems" (also called "body cams" or "cop cams") are small, pager-sized cameras that clip on to an officer's uniform or are worn as a headset and record audio and video of the officer's interactions with the public. Recent surveys suggest that about 25% of the nation's 17,000 police agencies were using them, with fully 80% of agencies evaluating the technology....

Although we at the ACLU [American Civil Liberties Union] generally take a dim view of the proliferation of surveillance cameras in American life, police on-body cameras are different because of their potential to serve as a check against the abuse of power by police officers. Historically, there was no documentary evidence of most encounters between police officers and the public, and due to the volatile nature of those encounters, this often resulted in radically divergent accounts of incidents. Cameras have the potential to be a win-win, helping protect the public against police misconduct and at the same time helping protect police against false accusations of abuse.

Jay Stanley, "Police Body-Mounted Cameras:
With Right Policies in Place, a Win for All,"
American Civil Liberties Union, March 2015.

With half of the police department wearing cameras recording each interaction with the public, the department experienced an 88 percent reduction in complaints against officers. Additionally, the study found that shifts without cameras experienced twice as many use-of-force incidents as shifts using the cameras.

Other studies conducted in Mesa, Arizona, and in the United Kingdom have also yielded promising results. Right now, police departments—including the Ferguson Police Department, and larger ones like the Los Angeles Police Department and Anaheim Police Department—are moving forward with pilot programs and trial runs for officers wearing body cameras. And other cities and locales in Southern California are exploring whether it would be feasible to start their use, as well.

A New Resource Pool

The biggest barrier that they face is funding.

I recently led an effort joined by thirty colleagues in the House—urging U.S. attorney general Eric Holder and the Department of Justice to help fund local police departments' purchase of small body-worn cameras. In Ferguson, the Department of Justice played an important role in defusing the situation in the immediate aftermath by bringing in community relations experts to create a dialogue as well as initiating its own civil rights investigation. The Justice Department can build on this effort by assisting police departments in acquiring body cameras.

For many departments, the cost of purchasing the cameras as well as the technical infrastructure needed to maintain them and store recorded footage is prohibitive. A variety of Department of Justice programs already provide equipment and financial support to local law enforcement agencies, and I believe a portion of that should be set aside for body cameras. The Department of Justice should also support rigorous, scientific study on the effects of camera adoption by police agencies as well [as] help to develop and disseminate best practices for their use.

These cameras will increase transparency, decrease tensions between police and community members, and create a record of events. The Department of Justice can use existing funding streams or work with Congress to create a new pool of resources for local governments to help implement body-worn cameras for police officers throughout the country.

This is an idea whose time has come—and it's time for the federal government to partner with local departments to make it happen.

> *"Cameras are not merely a distraction from the police accountability movement's underlying aims, but could actively set it back."*

Body Cameras Will Not Stop Police Brutality

Shahid Buttar

In the following viewpoint, Shahid Buttar argues that body cameras will not stop police brutality. Police may claim ownership of footage, preventing the public from ever seeing it, while cameras themselves could only increase surveillance of innocent Americans. It is better, Buttar believes, to reform police actions. Buttar is a constitutional lawyer and executive director of the Bill of Rights Defense Committee.

As you read, consider the following questions:

1. What does Buttar say is the real problem that allows police violence to continue?

2. According to Buttar, how could police body cameras fuel mass incarceration?

3. What does Buttar suggest the president should do to reduce police violence?

Recent evasions of justice by the NYPD [New York City Police Department] officers who killed Eric Garner prove what Americans of color have long known: Police can do anything—even murder someone in broad daylight on videotape, without provocation, using methods of force already held illegal—and get away with it.

Americans from all walks of life have responded with a rising tide of protests around the country, ranging from sit-ins at shopping malls and walkouts on college campuses to the occupation of train stations, major intersections and highways.

This movement for justice has largely untapped opportunities among potential allies and also faces a disturbing threat in proposals to expand the use of police body cameras.

A Movement to Which Washington Is Responding

The movement's visibility and assertiveness have already compelled a response from Washington. Policy proposals responding to the movement, however, threaten to distract from its most crucial goals, undermine its interests, and ultimately exacerbate mass incarceration.

After greeting grassroots organizers from Ferguson [Missouri, where Michael Brown, an unarmed, young black man was shot and killed by a police officer] at the White House, and affirming his concerns about the "militarized culture" of domestic police forces, President [Barack] Obama proposed to spend a quarter billion dollars on solutions including police body cameras. Body cameras, however, are no solution to the problem.

The real problem—which the president and Congress continue to ignore—is a legal system granting police broad latitude to commit civil rights violations. Between Congress amending it and courts interpreting it, the law must change so that police face justice for arbitrary violence, whether their human rights abuses happen on or off camera.

Cameras Promise Transparency but Don't Deliver

The parents of Mike Brown endorsed a call for body cameras because the facts surrounding their son's death have been in dispute since the day he was killed. Transparency is not sufficient without reform, nor is it ensured by cameras.

First, there's no guarantee that the public will ever see footage from police body cameras, especially in cases where it may be helpful to defendants or civil litigants.

When police have been observed filming demonstrations, for instance, civil litigants have been unable to gain access to footage in discovery due to self-serving police claims (not unlike the CIA's [Central Intelligence Agency's] claims when evading accountability for human rights abuses like torture) that the footage was either lost, recorded over, or never captured in the first instance.

Second, even when body camera footage is public, it remains an inadequate solution at best. Cameras captured video of Eric Garner's death, which millions of people watched on YouTube. But video neither saved Eric Garner nor helped hold his murderers accountable.

Moreover, even when everything does work as their proponents suggest, body cameras offer transparency only into particular incidents, not into patterns or practices.

A few weeks ago, when I testified before the Washington, DC, city council on policing reforms, members were eager to define what few statistics they could glean from the Metropolitan Police Department. In New York City, the council fought for a year merely to gain some insight into the racial impacts of NYPD stops, searches, surveillance and uses of force, through the creation of a new inspector general's office.

We need transparency into patterns and practices, not only into discrete acts.

Cameras Could Make Mass Incarceration Even Worse

Beyond failing to satisfy transparency concerns, police body cameras also pose a massive risk to privacy and could support mass incarceration. In these ways, cameras are not merely a distraction from the police accountability movement's underlying aims, but could actively set it back.

First, body cameras are oriented not toward police officers but rather toward the public. Nor are they particularly focused.

Rather than specifically capture footage of people involved in police encounters, body cameras monitor anyone within their field of vision, without the individual basis for suspicion constitutionally required to justify a police search. The president's body camera proposal would ultimately expand government surveillance of people suspected of no crime without doing much to check or balance police abuses.

By extending surveillance, cameras could also fuel mass incarceration. Cameras could capture footage used against defendants in criminal trials—either where the footage depicts criminal acts, like jaywalking or selling loose cigarettes, or where it merely supports suspicion of potential crime, justifying subsequent stops and searches that would otherwise be illegal.

It would be disturbing indeed for calls that "Black Lives Matter" to be answered with tools ensuring that they will continue to be treated as fodder for a corrupt system promoting racial injustice.

Cons of Police Body Cameras

In this techno-savvy age of the smartphone where almost anyone can record live events in real time, the question of on-duty police officers using body-mounted cameras to capture incidents as they unfold has come under intense scrutiny. The practice of using body-worn cams is in the initial stages of evaluation and study, although they are quickly becoming standard equipment in departments across the United States.

Following is a partial list of the cons and disadvantages:

- According to early versions of policies governing their use, law enforcement officers must physically activate the camera when they exit their patrol car. The recording equipment must be manually activated when interacting with civilians or recording statements during investigations. However, officers decide when to activate the camera, and for how long the footage is stored, and if and when it should be made accessible to the public. . . .

- Privacy issues are of concern for both cops and civilians. How to deal with those concerns is still being evaluated.

- Use of body cameras may prevent people from coming forward as credible witnesses to help assist with investigations, due to fear of retaliation or fear of public exposure.

- Technological issues related to the cameras may prevent proper functioning at times. This could be due to a dead battery, damaged components, obstructed lens, and other problems.

"Police Body Cameras: Do They Reduce Complaints of Officer Misconduct?," eInvestigator.com.

Real Solutions

In Ferguson, community members have compiled a sensible set of comprehensive demands, ranging from the adoption of federal legislation to end racial profiling to local measures ensuring accountability for rogue police officers, protections to give journalists and community members the right to observe police activities, and limits on military equipment acquisition.

The End Racial Profiling Act (ERPA)—included among the community's demands in Ferguson—would address the problem by requiring police departments to track and disclose the impacts of police activities. It would establish the transparency that body cameras promise but fail to deliver.

ERPA would not only enable transparency into patterns and practices, it would go further by creating a right of private action so survivors of profiling could seek their day in court. Under a disparate impact standard, plaintiffs could use the statistical evidence required from police to establish a discrimination claim without having to somehow prove an officer's specific intent to discriminate, as required under current federal law.

Washington Failing America, Yet Again

This is an issue on which both major political parties have failed America. ERPA was endorsed by the [George W.] Bush administration as early as 2001, years before President Obama came to Washington.

Yet, more than a decade later, the bill remains under the congressional bus, ignored by Republicans and Democrats alike. During the two years that Democrats most recently controlled the Senate, the bill did not receive a single hearing—even though profiling sparked a raging national controversy.

If the president can mobilize a quarter billion dollars to fund potential solutions to police violence in communities, those funds should go where they can most help. *Instead of further inflating the budgets of police departments, the president should invest in communities seeking job training, violence prevention, and youth counseling programs.*

Even if the goal remains unfortunately limited to establishing greater visibility into discrete police activities, and cameras are incorrectly perceived as the solution, the best way to get them on the streets is to train community members and aspiring citizen journalists.

Cameras fail to provide meaningful transparency, extend domestic spying, make mass incarceration even worse and represent a budgetary bonus to police departments and corporate camera contractors, while distracting the debate from the more important issue of officer—and department—accountability for abusive patterns and practices.

If the president wants to do more than pay lip service to the movement, he should endorse ERPA and push Congress to finally enact it.

In the meantime, seemingly spontaneous mass demonstrations will continue across the country. The movement to end police murder with impunity is not asking for new solutions. It has already put solutions on the table.

It's time to give Garner, Brown and all the other victims of police violence the justice they were denied during their lives and help them rest in peace by taking meaningful steps to ensure that police do not force others into their unfortunate footsteps.

> *"Time after time, the ability to record police-civilian interactions . . . has done less to deter police violence than to document it."*

Body Cameras Are Helpful but Insufficient for Stopping Police Brutality

Matthew Kovac

In the following viewpoint, Matthew Kovac contends that body cameras can document police brutality but cannot stop it. He cites the case of Eric Garner, who was recorded in an alleged choke hold by a police officer that killed him, but the officer was not indicted, despite video evidence of the act. Real solutions, Kovac believes, involve communities becoming focused on the safety of their neighborhoods. Kovac is a writer for the Youth Project.

As you read, consider the following questions:

1. Which three consequences does Kovac say camera footage usually leads to for abusive police?

2. According to Kovac, what controversy arose in Indiana over a new law regarding use of force against some police?

3. How does Kovac say programs such as Cure Violence can make neighborhoods safer?

When the death of Eric Garner at the hands of NYPD [New York City Police Department] officers was ruled a homicide earlier this month [August 2014], the response from the police union was as swift as it was predictable.

Just as police in Ferguson, Missouri, claim that unarmed African American teen Michael Brown brought about his own death by attacking an officer, the New York City Patrolmen's Benevolent Association [PBA] blamed the victim.

"We believe, however, that if he had not resisted the lawful order of the police officers placing him under arrest, this tragedy would not have occurred," PBA president Patrick Lynch said in a statement on Garner's death.

Yet this is far from what video of the incident showed. At more than six feet and 350 pounds, Garner could have easily shaken off his attackers. He didn't die because he resisted. He died because he didn't. Watching over the screens of their cell phones, neither did bystanders.

And who can blame them? They had, after all, just watched a man lose his life over the suspicion that he was selling untaxed cigarettes. They knew what would happen if they made a move. As did Garner, a 43-year-old father of six, who tried to go quietly despite his physical advantage.

In Ferguson, where protests and riots in the wake of Brown's death have been met with tear gas and rubber bullets, witnesses maintain that Brown, too, did nothing to provoke the altercation that ended his life, and that he had his hands up when he was shot dead.

That Garner and Brown could be killed with impunity in front of horrified onlookers is only the latest demonstration that grassroots efforts have failed to stem the nation's police brutality epidemic, which saw another unarmed black man killed Monday in Los Angeles.

The situation is especially dire in Chicago, where the city government has spent more than $500 million handling police misconduct cases since 2004, according to an April investigation by the Better Government Association.

Accountability, Not Deterrence

Time after time, the ability to record police-civilian interactions—usually seen as a victory for police accountability—has done less to deter police violence than to document it.

Sometimes this evidence results in police being held responsible for misconduct. Far more often, it leads to procedural slaps on the wrist, reduced charges, and lenient sentences.

In one particularly egregious case, Cook County prosecutors decided last November not to bring charges against an officer who was recorded fatally shooting an unarmed man in the back.

Whatever the courts decide to do with such evidence, it can't bring back the dead.

The nightly news hails as heroes those who intervene to stop crimes: ordinary citizens who foil a mugging or interrupt an assault. But what are people supposed to do when the perpetrators are police officers?

It is long past time to move from an after-the-fact accountability paradigm to initiatives focused on violence prevention and intervention.

In the wake of these deaths, the most pressing question is not how to reform police rules of engagement, or even whether civilian-elected police accountability councils—advocated by the Chicago Alliance Against Racist and Political Repression, among others—would put a dent in police forces' culture of impunity.

It's how people can be empowered to intervene in crimes when the criminals are wearing badges.

Such changes are unlikely to come through official channels. When Indiana amended its self-defense law in 2012 to allow the use of force against officers in some circumstances, it was only after a bitter fight with the police lobby, which claimed the law declared open season on police.

For communities of color across the country, of course, it has always been open season. In Chicago, African Americans are 10 times more likely to be shot by police than their white counterparts, according to a January analysis by the *Chicago Reporter*'s Angela Caputo.

Community Solutions

So what can ordinary people do to put the brakes on police violence?

Local media should end the age-old practice of the police blotter, which uncritically parrots charges like "resisting arrest" or "aggravated battery" without bothering to verify police claims. All charges should be thoroughly investigated, with comment given to defendants and witnesses.

Support networks could be organized to pay for the legal defense of those who intervene in police brutality incidents—and, more likely than not, their hospital bills.

Such steps could give communities the breathing room necessary to organize in their collective self-defense. In the 1960s, the Black Panther Party famously organized its own neighborhood patrols, tailing squad cars in an effort to deter police misconduct.

Another relevant, if controversial, approach is offered by Cure Violence, which mobilizes former gang members to "interrupt" shootings in their neighborhoods. Similar initiatives against police abuse, featuring community members and concerned ex-police and ex-military, could help curb violence.

The Black Panther Party for Self-Defense

Formed in 1966, the Black Panther Party for Self-Defense was the largest black revolutionary organization that has ever existed. . . .

Such was their success that they rapidly grew to a size of 5,000 full-time party workers, organized in 45 chapters (branches) across America. At their peak, they sold 250,000 papers every week. Opinion polls of the day showed the Panthers to have 90% support among blacks in the major cities. Their impact on black America can be measured by the response of the state. J. Edgar Hoover, then head of the FBI [Federal Bureau of Investigation], described them as "the number one threat to the internal security of the United States." . . .

The Panthers decided to take up their constitutional right to carry arms and to implement [civil rights activist] Malcolm X's philosophy of self-defense by patrolling the police. They did this at a time when severe police brutality was common—the police would beat down and kill blacks at random. They would even recruit police from the racist South to come and work in the northern ghettos.

On one occasion, whilst on patrol, they witnessed an officer stop and search a young guy. The Panthers got out of their car and went over to the scene and stood watching, their guns on full display. Angrily, the policeman began to question them and tried to intimidate them with threats of arrest. But [Black Panther cofounder] Huey P. Newton had studied the law intimately and could quote every law and court ruling relevant to their situation.

Adrian Wood and Nutan Rajguru,
"The Black Panther Party for Self-Defense," Socialist Alternative.

These measures alone will not end police brutality. For that to happen, there would need to be a fundamental restructuring of the social and economic order the police serve to uphold.

But they may be just enough to make officers think twice about using lethal force over a few untaxed cigarettes.

> "The murders of the two NYPD officers were ghastly, but no group of Americans should be asked to stop exercising their constitutional rights."

Americans Must Continue Protesting Police Brutality

Juan Thompson

In the following viewpoint, Juan Thompson argues that although the deaths of American civilians and police officers alike are worth grieving, no one should be requested to stop protesting against police brutality. African Americans especially, Thompson believes, deserve to continue doing this, as they have historically been treated poorly by America's police. Thompson is a journalist for the Intercept news site.

As you read, consider the following questions:

1. What statement about police by US attorney general Eric Holder and New York City mayor Bill de Blasio does Thompson say was exaggerated and attacked by conservatives?

2. What does Thompson say is wrong with the family of Michael Brown in Missouri commenting on the murders of two New York City police officers?

3. Aside from Brown and Eric Garner, what two other deceased African Americans does Thompson reference in connection to police brutality?

Last summer [June 2014], Jerad and Amanda Miller walked into a CiCi's Pizza restaurant in Las Vegas and murdered two police officers who were sitting down and having lunch. Jerad Miller pulled out a handgun and shot one officer in the back of his head, and before the other officer could react, Miller shot him in the throat. Amanda then joined in, as the couple lit up the incapacitated officers. Afterwards, the Millers placed the deceased bodies on the floor and covered them with a Gadsden flag and a swastika. The former, a Revolutionary War–era flag adopted by libertarian groups, is important because the Millers were rabid antigovernment activists, whose history of extremism was well documented. Video also surfaced showing the pair protesting at Cliven Bundy's ranch.

Bundy is the Nevada rancher who since 1993 has refused to pay grazing fees. He is also the man who alluded to possibly happier times when Negroes were slaves and had, he said, more freedom. The standoff between him and the government became a cri de coeur [passionate outcry] of antigovernment, right-wing activists. Yet there was no mass outcry, after the Millers murdered those two officers, against Bundy, his supporters, cable news, or Tea Party groups (the occasional pundit notwithstanding). There were certainly no calls for a cessation of First Amendment rights.

Fast-forward to Saturday [December 20, 2014], when Ismaaiyl Abdullah Brinsley killed two New York police officers as they sat in a marked patrol car outside a housing project in Bedford-Stuyvesant. Brinsley, who had long struggled with mental illness, tied the shootings on social media to the death of Eric Garner, who died in a choke hold during a confrontation with New York police officers.

Putting Aside Protest

The outrage machine was ready and salivating. The George Patakis, Rudy Giulianis and Pat Lynches of the world had been waiting for something like this to happen, so they could lash out at those they view as their enemies. Pataki, the Republican former New York governor, took to Twitter and blamed the police shootings on the supposed anti-cop rhetoric of outgoing U.S. attorney general Eric Holder and liberal New York mayor Bill de Blasio. I could not recall any anti-cop musings from Holder and de Blasio, so I went back and searched. They said, in essence, that America's police departments have a history of targeting and violating black people. That is it. But since we live in a country where police officers are so highly respected and immune to criticism—even when they are recorded doing something wrong—de Blasio's timid remarks qualify as anti-cop.

Lynch, the fanatical president of the NYPD [New York City Police Department] union, even went so far to accuse de Blasio of having the dead officers' blood on his hands. Meanwhile, Giuliani—who has reemerged from his reprobate business dealings to reclaim his role as America's reigning racial arsonist—blamed Barack Obama. "They [Obama and de Blasio] have created an atmosphere of severe, strong, antipolice hatred in certain communities. For that, they should be ashamed of themselves," he said on Fox News.

The family of Michael Brown, the widely mourned Ferguson, Missouri, police shooting victim, put out a statement that condemned the killings. It's hard to think of why a Midwestern family a time zone away should have to comment on a shooting in New York, other than that black Americans are always thought to be responsible—somehow, some way—for crimes to which they have no connection. As one Twitter user posted Saturday, "Only in America does the still-grieving family of a murdered black child have to come out with a statement about an unrelated crime." And Garner's daughter visited a memorial set up for the slain officers. Did NYPD commissioner Bill Bratton visit Garner's makeshift memorial? Did de Blasio?

The lives of the officers killed in Brooklyn were no more valuable or precious than those of Garner or Brown, to say nothing of Tamir Rice (fatally shot by police at age 12 while playing with a toy gun) or John Crawford (fatally shot while walking through Walmart with a BB gun). But today an apparently cowed de Blasio called for the protests, which were spawned by the killings of the aforementioned black males, to stop. "Put aside protest," he said, "put aside demonstrations, until these funerals are passed. Let's just focus on these families and what they have lost."

Stop protesting police brutality. Stop demanding racial justice. Stop fighting for black life.

The murders of the two NYPD officers were ghastly, but no group of Americans should be asked to stop exercising their constitutional rights because of what occurred in Brooklyn. This is particularly true for black Americans who have long been admonished to wait their turn. Black citizens are always expected to give up so much for a country that has given them so little. But two weeks ago New York activists organized a giant demonstration to protest police brutality.

I marched for seven hours in the city I now call home. In front of me, for a chunk of that time, was a father and his son. The son appeared to be 3 or 4 years old. At one point we passed a phalanx of NYPD officers whom the father promptly flipped off. He then looked down at his son, while motioning to the massive crowd, and said, simply, "This is for you." And so, despite Saturday's horrible events, black lives *still* matter.

> *"It's ... time to stop the bashing of law enforcement officers. They deserve our support."*

Americans Should Value, Not Protest, the Police

Charlie Dent

In the following viewpoint, Charlie Dent argues that despite how Americans may feel about various incidents of brutality against citizens, no one should protest the police, for they perform a dangerous duty for their communities. A better idea, he believes, is to work to build trust between police and the people they protect so that all parties receive the respect they deserve. Dent is the US congressman for Pennsylvania's fifteenth district.

As you read, consider the following questions:

1. What sequence of events does Dent say rightly led to the Missouri grand jury's decision not to indict Officer Darren Wilson for killing Michael Brown?

2. According to Dent, how should the makeup of police departments change?

Charlie Dent, "Op-Ed—Stop Bashing the Police," Charlie Dent, United States Congressman, January 6, 2015. Courtesy of Congressman Charlie Dent.

3. How does Dent say New York mayor Bill de Blasio is responsible for American protests against police?

The beautiful autumn foliage of Pennsylvania's Pocono Mountains served as the backdrop for several weeks of tension and fear during the massive manhunt for survivalist and cop killer Eric Frein. Frein ambushed and killed State Police Corporal Bryon Dickson II and seriously wounded Trooper Alex T. Douglass. Pennsylvanians are still coping with the tragedy, as are the devastated families of the two officers.

Perhaps Frein's recent murderous attack is why the horrific December 20th [2014] ambush and assassination of two New York City police officers, Rafael Ramos and Wenjian Liu, has caused many Pennsylvanians' hearts to break for the families of these two public servants, targeted simply because they wore the NYPD [New York City Police Department] uniform. Officer Ramos, a devoted husband and father of two young children, celebrated his 40th birthday earlier this month. Officer Liu, who married two months ago, leaves behind his devastated young wife and parents.

The assassination of Officers Ramos and Liu marks a critical moment in this nation's recent discussions on police practices and race relations in the aftermath of the deaths of Michael Brown and Eric Garner.

As a nation, how do we make sense of the events, especially since grand juries in Missouri and New York, after reviewing the evidence, declined to indict either of the officers involved?

As a father of three, I can't imagine losing a child under any circumstances. Yet, Michael Brown engaged in multiple criminal actions on that fateful day. Robbing a store (on video), defying a police order to get on the sidewalk and out of the middle of the street, resisting arrest, attempting to take Officer [Darren] Wilson's firearm (which discharged during the altercation) and then rushing at that same officer are facts corroborated by multiple witnesses and supported by forensic evidence. Given these facts, the grand jury made the right decision not to indict Officer Wilson.

Out of this tragic event came the wanton destruction of the Ferguson riots, the "hands up, don't shoot" protests, the undue vilification of Officer Wilson, and the unhelpful lectures from discredited provocateur Al Sharpton.

No Reasonable Pretext

The circumstances of Eric Garner's death are also complex and tragic. While the video image of Mr. Garner's arrest is disturbing, a grand jury decided not to indict the NYPD officer in question. Reasonable people can disagree about the grand jury's decision, but that was their informed judgment after hearing the arguments and seeing all the evidence. No one should die for selling "loose" cigarettes.

However, the cases of Brown and Garner do not provide a reasonable pretext to end the highly effective "broken windows" police practices or to prohibit local police from buying military surplus protective gear and other equipment. Absolutely neither justifies the actions of some New York protestors, despicably caught on video, chanting: "What do we want? Dead cops! When do we want them? Now!"

Police work is inherently dangerous. Officers must enforce the law in any number of difficult situations under pressures few outside of the military could possibly understand. From routine traffic stops to domestic violence situations to hostage cases to murder scenes, America's finest deal with it all. It's past time to stop the bashing of law enforcement officers. They deserve our support. They certainly have mine.

It is necessary to engage in a conversation to discuss the fears of those in the African American community about their relationship with law enforcement. Efforts to build a sense of teamwork and trust between law enforcement and residents of neighborhoods experiencing high crime rates must be made.

A Lack of Diversity

None of the metro area's most racially diverse cities—Grandview, Raytown, and the two Kansas Cities—has enough minority officers on its force to mirror its community's racial makeup.

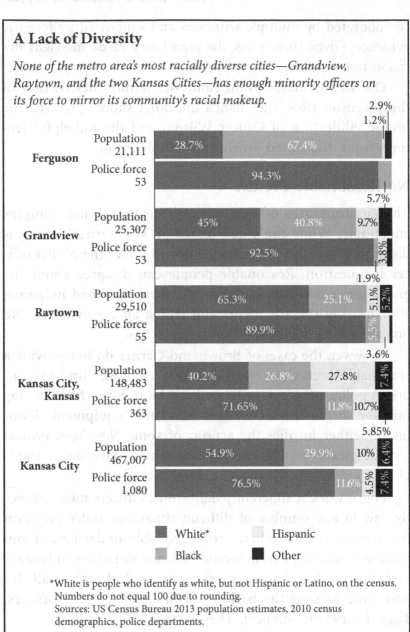

White* Hispanic Black Other

*White is people who identify as white, but not Hispanic or Latino, on the census. Numbers do not equal 100 due to rounding.
Sources: US Census Bureau 2013 population estimates, 2010 census demographics, police departments.

TAKEN FROM: Glenn E. Rice and Tony Rizzo, "Like Ferguson, Area Police Departments Lack Racial Diversity," *Kansas City Star*, August 23, 2014.

Moreover, the makeup of police departments should reflect the people and communities they serve.

Respected Public Servants

As the nation comes to grips with the deaths of Officers Ramos and Liu, New York mayor Bill de Blasio should be held to account for his antipolice campaign rhetoric and tacit approval of the protests against his police department, which is not only diverse but among the finest big-city police forces anywhere in the world. The indelible image of New York police officers turning their backs on the mayor—on two separate high-profile occasions—should be cause for him to reflect and do some serious soul-searching. Mayor de Blasio is perceived by many in the NYPD, as well as the broader community nationally, as hostile to the very public servants New Yorkers rely upon to keep their city safe.

Mayor de Blasio is not responsible for the deaths of the two officers; gunman Ismaaiyl Brinsley is solely responsible. However, the mayor's words and actions have contributed to an antipolice atmosphere, not only in his city but also around the nation. If he's wise, the mayor will work to repair his relationship with the men and women of the NYPD. An apology from the mayor to the NYPD regarding some of his recent statements would be a constructive first step.

Anyone who has ever attended a local crime watch meeting knows that police officers care deeply about the communities they serve. I've attended many of these over the years, and the officers have immersed themselves in the daily life of the neighborhoods for which they are responsible.

It's about time the national media narrative start to reflect this reality and treat police officers with the respect they have earned. Now is the time for us all to roll up our sleeves and work to address the underlying issues that have animated enormous emotion in communities across our country.

> "I am proposing that the legal authority that's now restricted to a single police department and stems from a local government be extended to multiple policing companies or voluntary organizations."

Civilian Oversight of Police Could Stop Brutality

Michael S. Rozeff

In the following viewpoint, Michael S. Rozeff argues that civilian involvement in policing could stop police brutality in America. He believes that citizens should be allowed to form their own police departments, which could then compete with badly performing police departments and even put them out of business. To Rozeff, with this kind of competition, abusive police would need to reform or be forced out of service. Rozeff is a writer for Lew rockwell.com.

As you read, consider the following questions:

1. According to Rozeff, what problem would result if the US Justice Department began to oversee local police forces?

2. What reasons does Rozeff give to explain why police forces perform badly?

3. What does Rozeff say is the difference between citizen police and vigilantes?

How can the behavior of police be improved?

Police departments throughout America have been documented generally to perform badly. One major report reads:

"Police abuse remains one of the most serious and divisive human rights violations in the United States. The excessive use of force by police officers, including unjustified shootings, severe beatings, fatal chokings, and rough treatment, persists because overwhelming barriers to accountability make it possible for officers who commit human rights violations to escape due punishment and often to repeat their offenses. Police or public officials greet each new report of brutality with denials or explain that the act was an aberration, while the administrative and criminal systems that should deter these abuses by holding officers accountable instead virtually guarantee them impunity."

This report's recommendations are for the federal government to monitor the local and state police departments and withhold funds if they perform badly. But it notes that the Justice Department already fails to do the monitoring it was empowered to do in 1994! Besides, there is no reason to believe that centralization of this kind will improve local behavior significantly. It will create another level of bureaucracy, another barrier for the complaints of citizens to find a court that provides sanctions and justice, and institute a backdoor method of nationalizing police forces that endangers liberty. We have already seen police brutality increase as the Pentagon has disbursed sophisticated weaponry and vehicles. We have already seen other federal agencies introducing their own police forces and using police state methods.

The solution is definitely not nationalization, federalization or centralization.

The problem with the current police forces is organizational. Police forces are local monopolies. This has historical roots in which governments came to be the sole sources of the authority for the police to wield their powers. "Local police includes municipal, county, tribal, and regional police that derive authority from the local governing body that created it."

It is because these police forces are monopolies and because they are linked to the courts and justice systems that they perform badly. This is why we read of their mismanagement, failures to be held accountable, brutality, failures to discipline badly performing officers, hiring brutes and failing to investigate their records, poor training, and so on. There are also related issues of police unions and political pressures. Only in a walled-off and protected environment can such bad behavior persist.

Radical Reorganization

My recommendation is the libertarian one and also the appropriate organizational one. The authority to perform police functions should not be allocated to a monopolistic police force. It should be devolved to citizens themselves who are allowed to form companies that offer police services to the public. They can also form volunteer forces, departments and innovate other methods of policing. In this way, positive market forces come into play. Poor policing that is recognized by the consuming public is sanctioned by their withdrawal of patronage from those groups or companies or departments offering them. Good policing is rewarded by gaining customers

"Special Police" Help Fight Crime

Michael Youlen stopped a driver in a Manassas, Virginia, apartment complex on a recent night and wrote the man a ticket for driving on a suspended license. With a badge on his chest and a gun on his hip, Youlen gave the driver a stern warning to stay off the road.

The stop was routine police work, except for one fact: Youlen is not a Manassas officer. The citation came courtesy of the private force he created that, until recently, he called the "Manassas Junction Police Department."

He is its chief and sole officer.

He is a force of one.

And he is not alone. Like more and more Virginians, Youlen gained his police powers using a little-known provision of state law that allows private citizens to petition the courts for the authority to carry a gun, display a badge and make arrests. The number of "special conservators of the peace"—or SCOPs, as they are known—has doubled in Virginia over the past decade to roughly 750, according to state records. . . .

In neighboring Washington, a similar designation called "special police" requires 40 hours of training. Maryland officials leave instruction to the discretion of employers but have no requirements. Other states have similar systems.

Justin Jouvenal,
"A Little-Known Virginia Law Is Letting Citizens Start
Their Own Police Force, Carry a Badge and Arrest People,"
Washington Post, *March 1, 2015.*

or subscribers or volunteers or participants. The policing offered by the local governments becomes one among many, no longer protected. Exposed to competition, it either shapes up or ships out.

Naturally, I recognize that this solution goes against an entrenched system that almost everyone takes for granted, the system of local monopolies. However, historical and legal precedents for citizen police authority exist. We have all heard of citizen arrests. We all know or should know that the American theory of government makes the people sovereign and the source of such power, not the governments. "Of the people, by the people and for the people," remember?

There is the problem that the local governments and police forces resist such changes. They tend to label serious policing by alternative groups as vigilantes. They raise scares that such forces and groups are unprofessional or need licensing and so on. Competition will be accused of creating a "Wild West." The answers to these baseless charges are many. For one thing, the Wild West was not the violent place it has been depicted as. But I will say no more in rebuttal in this short blog, other than that those who claim to be professional are way too frequently behaving worse than vigilantes. Citizen review boards and other such monitoring or quasi-judicial groups apparently are either toothless, too slow, or captured by pro-police personnel to solve the mushrooming problems of police in America. A vigilante is someone who appoints himself to law enforcement without legal authority. That is not what I am proposing. I am proposing that the legal authority that's now restricted to a single police department and stems from a local government be extended to multiple policing companies or voluntary organizations, not licensed but freely chartered to undertake policing functions.

For a simpler idea of this, just imagine that wherever you live, you can phone any one of several police departments, not just one. If you live in an area with several towns nearby, you could call any one of them. You are no longer restricted and neither are they; they can operate wherever people call them. This places them in competition and immediately changes the incentives they face. If you live in a large city that has one big police department, imagine breaking it up into several that can operate anywhere. Then you could call any one of these. They could be run on a profit-making basis or a volunteer basis or both side by side.

Criminal violence arises from criminal behavior, whether that of people doing criminal acts, career criminals, or police behaving criminally. It only becomes a routine or widespread attribute of policing forces, whose aim is supposed to be anti-criminal, when those policing forces possess unaccountable or weakly accountable powers. That's the case in many of today's monopolistic police departments. Competition will bring those perverse behaviors under control and reduce them, by the power of people's purses who are buying the policing services.

VIEWPOINT

| *"It's very difficult to establish oversight over [police] because they view it as an us-against-them framework."*

Civilian Oversight of Police Has Benefits and Disadvantages

Pete Eyre

In the following viewpoint, Pete Eyre, speaking with Brian Buchner, Pamela J. Meanes, and Jonathan S. Taylor, argues that citizen oversight of police would present numerous advantages and disadvantages. Such a change, the speakers believe, would bring accountability to police departments that formerly abused their authority. However, police would probably resist this implementation strongly, as they have long enjoyed governing themselves. Eyre is cofounder of the Cop Block organization.

As you read, consider the following questions:

1. What does Jonathan S. Taylor say is a major restriction placed on citizen oversight of police?

2. What does Eyre dislike about including the term "citizen" in the names of police oversight boards?

3. What does Brian Buchner say would be one major obstacle to implementing civilian oversight of police?

Particularly since Michael Brown's death at the hands of police in Ferguson, Missouri, a national dialogue has been taking place regarding the creation of citizen oversight boards to monitor law enforcement. In this, the fifth installment of *Fatal Encounters*, the *Reno News & Review*'s [RN&R's] series on issues of deadly police violence, we've assembled a panel of people who, for various reasons, have reached the national stage with regard to police violence.

Our panel includes Brian Buchner, president of NACOLE, National Association for Civilian Oversight of Law Enforcement, which has engaged with the city of Ferguson to develop a new citizen oversight committee in that community. Pete Eyre is cofounder of Cop Block, a national decentralized project that focuses on police accountability. Pamela J. Meanes is president of the National Bar Association and active in the recent actions in Ferguson, Missouri. Jonathan S. Taylor is a professor at California State University, Fullerton, who's been active in issues of police violence, particularly following the brutal crackdown on the Occupy movement and the killing of the mentally ill man Kelly Thomas in 2011.

Oversight Advantages

RN&R: What are the benefits to civilian oversight of law enforcement?

Buchner: There are a number of benefits to civilian oversight of law enforcement. Civilian oversight helps support effective policing. Civilian oversight helps build bridges between the police department and the community that it serves. It ensures greater accountability and transparency in policing. It helps manage risk inside an agency and within the jurisdiction. And related to building trust and building bridges, it helps increase confidence in the police department.

Eyre: My initial thought is that I would think that we would all have a shared end goal, which is to live free. I could use civilian oversight to maybe have less corruption or double standards applied to people who violate the rights of others who happen to be aggressive with badges and things like that. The thought I had was, why do we want to build a bridge to this institution? Essentially, we're just changing the deck chairs on a boat that's sinking. It's the institution that needs to change. I'd just advocate that we move past the institution and build something different altogether that would bring about the desirable conclusion.

Meanes: I don't know what the benefits are of police review boards, because of the ones that we've taken a look at, the citizens have complained that those have become an extension of the police department. Sometimes, there is an appearance that the police still are unable—even through the review boards—to police themselves. I think it's better to have some type of independent federal oversight and an independent evaluation. Or if there is a police review board or some type of citizen oversight board, that that board is really represented by the citizens and not necessarily by individuals who may be somehow connected to the department.

RN&R: Jonathan, would you respond to the question? What are the benefits to civilian oversight?

Taylor: Accountability, of course, that's the goal, but I think we have to look beyond that. We have to look at the big picture, the long-term goal. I think the goal should be to end or reduce police violence as much as possible. Civilian oversight is one tool that can be used to help reduce police violence, but I also think it's insufficient in and of itself. There are many issues involved with police violence, and civilian oversight will only go so far. Where I live in California, civilian oversight is only as useful as the law permits it to be. In

California, because of laws that protect police officer confidentiality, it's just not that useful. So, yeah it's much better to have a police oversight committee than to not have one because any sort of civilian control over the police is preferable to none. But there are a bunch of structural obstacles to having it really work.

RN&R: Didn't some changes come about in your neck of the woods after Kelly Thomas?

Taylor: No, not really. There were no substantive changes. There's probably a lower level of blatant police violence in the city of Fullerton itself, but that's more the result of the protests and the fact that the community sort of had an uprising. There still is no civilian oversight board or authority in Fullerton at all. There's a committee that's been trying to get civilian oversight, but there is no civilian oversight yet.

Buchner: I'm going to push back on that just a little bit because the city did contract with an organization called the Office of Independent Review Group, OIR Group. I think they're calling it an independent auditor—and that independent auditor is charged with a number of things, including use-of-force investigations, samples of complaints, and conducting independent audits of police department investigations and activities. There was a committee of concerned citizens called the Police Oversight Proposal Committee, and they were pushing for something other than was ultimately adopted, but as a result of that discussion, the city did contract with this OIR Group for that independent audit function for a couple of years, actually using asset forfeiture funds, which is kind of unique in the world of civilian oversight.

Taylor: I was at the city council meeting when Michael Gennaco gave his report and presented the findings. The general take on that in the city of Fullerton from the community was that was a whitewash, and that his office is essentially contracted in order to prevent meaningful oversight, so it's a sort of smoke screen. Of course there are going to be different takes on this—it's just a matter of perspective—but the people that I know who are critical of the police in Fullerton did not view the hiring of the OIR Group as true oversight in any sense. We feel that that's just kind of window dressing, and there really haven't been very meaningful changes.

RN&R: Pete, do you want to respond to the original question? What are the benefits to civilian oversight?

Eyre: I would just add to what I initially stated. I personally have issues that we would be likened to a citizen because a "citizen" implies that there are two classes of people—the citizens and the noncitizens, and then inevitably there are then two sets of rights that apply. I believe that each person is equal no matter where on Earth they were born, no matter what color, no matter any of those arbitrary characteristics. As Jon [Taylor] noted, yes, it is preferable to have one than not to have one, but I don't think it's a worthy allocation of resources. I think that law enforcement exists ostensibly to provide effective safety or security, and I think that those, like in any other good or service, could better be provided through consensual interactions. Instead of trying to put a Band-Aid on this corrupt system, I would rather we just move past it and create something better.

Buchner: One of the things that we see across the country is that people have different understandings of what civilian oversight of law enforcement is and what it looks like. And so some people think of civilian oversight as a civilian review board or some kind of police commission, and maybe it would be helpful to start off either with a definition or some kind of common understanding.

Civilian Organization

RN&R: We could address that in the next question, which is, what should civilian oversight look like? For example, should oversight primarily focus on after-the-fact things like misconduct or officer-involved violence, should it be more concerned with more proactive ideals like transparency and policy setting, should it be entirely independent to investigate anything it chooses, or are there better strategies?

Buchner: The definition that we use is one that's being kind of adopted from Dr. Sam Walker who's one of the noted scholars on civilian oversight, probably over the last 20 years. We define it as "an agency or procedure that involves participation by persons who are not sworn officers. They investigate, audit or review internal police investigations or processes including citizen complaints and use of force in incidents. And they conduct ongoing monitoring of law enforcement agencies, policies, procedures, training and management supervision practices." So it's a pretty broad definition that really means non–law enforcement officers have some role in overseeing the conduct operations or activities of a law enforcement agency.

Meanes: I think citizen oversight would have to be a combination of a few of those things in order to return some credibility and some trust back to the community. I think the oversight or the individuals doing the oversight need to have the freedom to independently issue opinion—similar to how you have attorney review boards—to determine whether or not a violation has occurred. That opinion should have some weight within the department to review and evaluate an officer. The review board should have the independent opportunity—not the same weight and force as Internal Affairs—but it should have some process to evaluate and monitor police misconduct investigations. It should not be looking just when misconduct happens, but it should be looking at the causes that may contribute to what happened and making some recommendations to the law enforcement agency, the community and the political officials: "Here are some things that we can do to be proactive instead of reactionary to things," because if the police review board is limited to just responding to issues that are raised about an officer or the department, then we're not going to get to a place where there is trust built between the citizens and the police force. The police review board becomes almost like a police entity within itself, and you don't want to create that. You do want the board's job really to be to create trust back between the community and the officers.

Oversight Obstacles

RN&R: What are the obstacles to having citizen oversight?

Taylor: I see a lot of obstacles. First of all, I see cultural obstacles. I think the police view themselves as a special protected class, different than the rest of the us, and with that kind of mentality it's very difficult to establish oversight over them because they view it as an us-against-them framework. I think they're sort of indoctrinated to feel that the people that they're dealing with are—they use the words like thugs and scumbags—and that people who are on drugs are always criminals. They have all these preconceptions based on the dominant model of police in the U.S. historically, and so I think there's a huge cultural obstacle to civilian oversight coming from within the mentality of police officers.

Then I think there are various political obstacles. I do think that cities and municipalities—all sorts of government—use police as revenue generators and so for civilians to come in and say, "No we don't want them to do this anymore," which is what I would do if I were on a police board, we're talking about cutting off their funding stream. Things like asset forfeiture, which I'm completely against in almost any capacity, that's their bread and butter, so there are economic motivations. There is a lot of organized power. Police unions are major lobbyists. Politicians are afraid to cross police unions, and therefore legislators write policies that benefit police unions that are essentially scripted by police unions. So you have these very major bureaucratic legal obstacles to civilian oversight. I view it as being almost impossible.

Eyre: I would echo a lot of what Jonathan [Taylor] said about the legal protections, such as sovereign immunity, which essentially equates to impunity. Ultimately, the biggest obstacle is ideas. The existing paradigm says that a certain group of people has a legal right to steal from others in their area and to then protect them. I think better ideas are assured, and those bad ideas will get shed in favor of better ideas. So currently the biggest obstacle is the bad idea that says that some people are authorities based on where they work instead of authorities based on having earned that authority. To me someone who claims to protect you, if they first steal from you, that doesn't grant them any authority in my book. Jonathan used the word "indoctrination" to apply to police employees, but I would also say that the folks who seek to control others have for decades used public school systems to essentially help shape the mind-sets of the people that they seek to control. Likewise the corporate media—you know that 95 percent of it is owned by six corporations now—it's much easier for these self-proclaimed leaders to have their messages peddled through those outlets. You almost never see a mainstream media source question police employees. They just quote them verbatim as if they speak the truth, and they afford them as authorities. So again, it's the ideas that have to change.

RN&R: OK, Brian, what's your idea of obstacles that exist to establishing civilian oversight?

Buchner: Jonathan [Taylor] said the obstacles are political, economic and social. I think those are some big points. I would just add that obstacles to establishing oversight and building and maintaining effective oversight include a failure to engage the community in a meaningful way. To get true public participation in the oversight of police, I think is a real obstacle. To say "community" in some ways is disingenuous because it implies that there's a unified community. We know that that's not the case.

There are different groups within every community and not every one of those groups is going to support police reform or to support oversight. I think to the extent that any community or city or county or jurisdiction is able to really get public participation and public input so that the model of oversight or the approach to oversight reflects and tries to maximize public interest while also realizing that there are other interests at play, I think is probably a big obstacle.

Periodical and Internet Sources Bibliography

The following articles have been selected to supplement the diverse views presented in this chapter.

Ginia Bellafante	"Police Violence Seems to Result in No Punishment," *New York Times*, December 4, 2014.
Mary Frances Berry	"Power to the People: Why We Need Civilian Police Review Boards," *Beacon Broadside*, February 11, 2015.
Stacia L. Brown	"Having Black Cops and Black Mayors Doesn't End Police Brutality," *New Republic*, April 29, 2015.
Kim Geiger	"Police Body Cameras Could Be Funded by $5 State Fee on Traffic Tickets," *Chicago Tribune*, May 28, 2015.
Justin Hansford	"Why Police Body Cameras Won't Work," *Hartford Courant*, December 5, 2014.
Martin Kaste	"Police Are Learning to Accept Civilian Oversight, but Distrust Lingers," NPR, February 21, 2015.
Ed Krayewski	"Four Police Brutality Reforms to Focus On: A Libertarian Take," Reason.com, September 2, 2014.
Steven Rosenfeld	"Plan on Protesting? What You Should Know About Your Rights and the Powers the Police Have," AlterNet, December 6, 2014.
Jonathan M. Smith	"Police Unions Must Not Block Reform," *New York Times*, May 29, 2015.
Alex S. Vitale	"Why Police Are Rarely Indicted for Misconduct," *Al Jazeera America*, November 24, 2014.

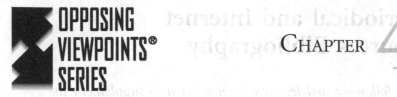

OPPOSING
VIEWPOINTS®
SERIES

CHAPTER 4

What Is the US Government's Response to Police Brutality?

Chapter Preface

The shooting death of Michael Brown by police officer Darren Wilson in Ferguson, Missouri, in August 2014 produced such a raucous national call for accountability for violent police that the federal Department of Justice (DOJ) announced that month that it would begin investigating the city police department for patterns of misconduct. Days later, representatives from three sections of the DOJ—including the Federal Bureau of Investigation (FBI), the Civil Rights Division, and the US attorney's office, as well as US attorney general Eric Holder himself—arrived in Ferguson and began poring through police records while gathering information from local witnesses about the events surrounding Brown's death. The goal of this was to expose and correct any consistent civil rights violations of Ferguson residents by city police and ultimately force the department to reform.

At the time of its Ferguson investigation, the DOJ was criticized by some national politicians for interfering in a local matter. Critics argued that state justice authorities should examine Ferguson police, not federal agents. In fact, the DOJ had been granted power to intervene in any smaller law enforcement entity that received federal funding by the 1994 Violent Crime Control and Law Enforcement Act. The DOJ's history as a national crime-fighting agency, however, dates to even earlier than this, with the American founders' Judiciary Act of 1789.

This law established the judicial branch of the US federal government, as prescribed in the US Constitution. In addition to the Supreme Court, the act created the Office of the Attorney General, who was to be a legal scholar responsible for defending the United States in federal court and advising the president on related matters. Despite these important duties, attorneys general were given no authority to form a department for themselves or even to employ staff to help them with their intense workloads.

The US Congress attempted numerous times to change this throughout the 1800s, but it took until 1870 for it to pass legislation that ultimately created the Department of Justice. This federal division would be overseen by the attorney general and a full team of legal aides and other assistants. Throughout the burgeoning modern era of the 1900s, attorneys general, by their work, became the visual figureheads of the entire American justice system, carrying out the wills of the individuals holding the office of president of the United States at the time. Therefore, today, despite the required impartiality of their legal undertakings, US attorneys general also represent the political persuasions of the president who appointed them.

Eric Holder became attorney general in 2009 under President Barack Obama. Both men stated that they cared deeply about the enforcement of civil rights in America. In 2014, then, Holder and his Justice Department enthusiastically began investigating possible civil rights violations by Ferguson police. The eventual DOJ report, published in March 2015, revealed that city police unconstitutionally targeted African Americans with unfair arrests, abuse, and other misconduct. While the American public harshly criticized the Ferguson Police Department for its activities, the DOJ, employing its authority as a federal agency, forced the department to begin reforming itself to engage in fair and constitutional policing practices.

The following chapter presents viewpoints relating to the US federal government's response to incidents of police brutality. Topics covered include the government's will to correct police brutality, President Obama's separation of racism from police violence, and the Department of Justice's ability to expose and reform police brutality.

> *"Giving criminals passes for their bad
> acts is not exactly what one expects to
> see from federal prosecutors."*

The Federal Government Is Failing to Correct Police Brutality

Barry Sussman

In the following viewpoint, Barry Sussman argues that the United States federal government is not holding abusive police officers accountable for their wrongful actions. Rather, it is attempting to reform their policing practices without punishing those responsible for committing crimes against citizens. Sussman believes this will inevitably lead to the perpetuation of police brutality in America. Sussman is a New Jersey attorney specializing in federal criminal procedure.

As you read, consider the following questions:

1. Why does Sussman say local prosecutors cannot be trusted to reprimand bad police?

2. What kinds of police misconduct does Sussman say were carried out by the Ferguson, Missouri, police department?

3. What percentage rate of conviction by federal prosecutors in court does Sussman label absurd?

The current epidemic of police violence aimed against the very citizens they are sworn to protect and serve shows no sign of abating. Just this past week [in March 2015] has focused attention on high-profile incidents involving the savage beating of a college honor student and the extrajudicial murder of a mentally ill man holding a screwdriver. These and countless similar incidents have exposed the motto "protect and serve" to be utterly Orwellian [referring to author George Orwell and used to describe situations that threaten the welfare of a free society], while severely diminishing how the public views law enforcement.

University of Virginia (UVA) honor student Martese Johnson was pummeled for no apparent reason by Alcohol Beverage Control (ABC) police near the UVA campus. His alleged offense is still unclear, but early reports, since refuted, claimed he was using a fake ID at a bar on St. Patrick's Day.

The ABC police were involved in another high-profile incident in 2013 involving the mistaken arrest of a female UVA student. In this incident Elizabeth Daly was approached by seven plainclothes ABC officers who drew at least one gun on the panicked student, believing the case of water she was carrying in her car was beer. Daly was arrested and held in prison overnight. She later received an undisclosed financial settlement reported to be as high as $200,000 as a result of her terrifying ordeal.

Dallas police gunned down Jason Harrison in his home after his mother called 911 requesting assistance with her son who had a history of mental problems. Harrison was holding a small screwdriver and despite officers' claims that he was "menacing" them with the screwdriver and that they were in fear of their lives, video released this week from an officer's body camera clearly contradicts these claims. The family has since filed a federal lawsuit against the city and offending officers claiming that Harrison posed no threat.

The American Civil Liberties Union (ACLU) recently filed an amicus brief in the U.S. Supreme Court arguing that hundreds of disabled Americans are killed in police encounters every year. . . . It was filed in support of a mentally ill woman suing San Francisco police for shooting her five times.

While police apologists seek to either justify every violent encounter or parrot the "99% of cops are good" mantra, elements of law enforcement continue to operate as a predatory street gang, ignoring their purported sworn duty. Executions are routinely justified by the officers claiming, as they did in the case of the Harrison murder, that they were "in fear of their lives."

Unlawful Bias

Local prosecutors, largely because of their symbiotic and incestuous relationship with police departments, have proven to be unwilling or unable to adequately police the police, so to speak. Typically when state and local agencies do not possess adequate resources to tackle a particular criminal matter, the Department of Justice (DOJ) finds a way to assume the lead and apply federal law. Yet federal prosecutors have been oddly reticent to impose the expansive federal criminal code to situations involving police misconduct.

Even in Ferguson, Missouri, which has been a flashpoint of tension between police and protestors since the summary execution of Michael Brown, the federal government has refused to address violative acts identified in the DOJ's own report. The report concluded that the Ferguson Police Department and the city's municipal court engaged in a "pattern and

practice" of discrimination against African Americans, disproportionately targeting them for traffic stops, use of force and
jail sentences. The report also includes the finding that
Ferguson's practices are shaped by the desire for revenue rather
than by public safety needs.

Even more insidious than the idea of forsaking public
safety for revenue generation was the report's conclusion that
the disproportionate number of arrests, tickets and use of
force stemmed from "unlawful bias," rather than black people
committing more crime. This was no mere bald assertion.
Specific instances of blatant police misconduct were included
in the DOJ's report. These items included illegal searches, unlawful arrests, beatings, unwarranted imprisonment, failure to
credit prisoners for time served, and the use of police dogs as
weapons against the public. The report concluded that in every dog bite incident reported, the person bitten was black.

The 105-page report could hardly have been more damning. A well-known and recognized police tactic to cover for
and justify meritless arrests is to claim the victim was "resisting arrest." The report detailed how from October 2012 to October 2014, every time a person was arrested in Ferguson for
resisting arrest, that person was black.

Yet despite the DOJ's outrageous findings of police criminality, no federal charges are pending, no federal grand jury
has been impaneled and there is little expectation of federal
charges being brought against the offending officers.

Attorney General Eric Holder has gone on record in citing
various illegalities on the part of the Ferguson Police Department. "According to our investigation, this emphasis on revenue generation through policing has fostered unconstitutional practices—or practices that contribute to constitutional
violations—at nearly every level of Ferguson's law enforcement system."

Police Handling of Mentally Ill Persons

A body-camera video of the June 2014 police shooting of a mentally ill Dallas [Texas] man has been released, showing the chilling moments that led to the man's death.

The family of Jason Harrison, a 38-year-old man who suffered from bipolar disorder and schizophrenia, released the graphic video Monday to show the public how the police handled the mentally ill man.

The video clip ... shows two officers responding to an Oak Cliff home on June 14, 2014....

The 38-year-old is seen standing in the doorway twirling a screwdriver in his hands. The officers, noticing the potential weapon, yell for the man to drop it as his mother is heard in the background screaming, 'Jay! Jay!'

Harrison appears to take a step away from the doorway and the two officers immediately fire at the man. In the video, a stun gun is seen in one of the officer's holsters but was never used to control Harrison....

Harrison stumbles toward the garage, covered in blood, and falls as his mother is heard yelling, 'You killed my child!' ...

In October, Harrison's family filed a wrongful death and violation of civil rights lawsuit against the officers, arguing that Harrison, who the family says was not a violent person, posed no threat to the cops, NBC reports.

However, the officers' attorney, Chris Livingston, says the men feared for their lives, the *Dallas Morning News* reports.

"Caught on Body Camera: The Chilling Moment Cops Shot
Dead Mentally Disabled Man Wielding a Screwdriver,"
Daily Mail, *March 17, 2015.*

Looking the Other Way

But Holder and the DOJ are dealing with the criminal elements within the Ferguson Police Department very differently than other armed gangs which prey upon the public. Instead of announcing arrests and indictments, Holder suggested that the Ferguson Police Department get residents more involved in policing decisions and implement better ways of tracking "stop, search, ticketing and arrest practices."

Giving criminals passes for their bad acts is not exactly what one expects to see from federal prosecutors who are typically not only enforcing every available criminal statute, but finding new and imaginative ways to criminalize an even wider array of behavior. After all, almost any prosecutor can obtain a conviction when there is a clear-cut violation of the law, but it takes an especially imaginative one to convict people for acts previously deemed to be compliant. Twisting existing criminal statutes beyond their intended purpose is one way in which federal prosecutors position themselves for advancement up the judicial corporate ladder.

No such creativity is needed to apply federal criminal law to predatory elements within law enforcement. Rampant unjustifiable assaults on citizens constitute rather clear violations of criminal law and can easily be prosecuted under the expansive and seemingly all-encompassing federal criminal code. There are a plethora of federal criminal statutes under which offending officers could potentially be successfully prosecuted, so many in fact that both Congress and the American Bar Association have been unsuccessful in compiling a complete list of every federal criminal violation. Yet Holder and the DOJ are inexplicably hesitant to devote resources to the prosecution of law enforcement personnel who violently break the law and violate the rights of others.

While federal prosecutors look the other way at police violence, they continue to vigorously prosecute a variety of minutia. Nearly three-quarters of all federal prisoners are serving time for nonviolent offenses, while approximately 35 percent are first-time, nonviolent offenders. Seemingly, no crime is too small for federal prosecutors to ignore.

Many commentators attempt to explain away the DOJ's failure to rein in rogue elements within law enforcement by citing a purported difficulty in bringing successful prosecutions against the police. Federal prosecutors currently enjoy an utterly absurd 99.5 percent rate of conviction in U.S. federal courts, at least in part due to the fact that many of the aforementioned federal "crimes" are little more than catchalls in that they can successfully be applied to almost any scenario a prosecutor wishes to target. The notion that there is some inherent difficulty in bringing federal prosecutions against violent offenders who happen to be committing their crimes under the color of law is laughable.

Despite their protestations of impotence in the face of blatant criminality, the decision of federal prosecutors to ignore criminal police action, a form of state-sponsored terrorism, is wholly arbitrary. Federal prosecutions tend to be arbitrary affairs in general, subject to the whims of prosecutors who typically select cases for prosecution based upon which will best strengthen their resume.

Federal prosecutors are trained to find criminality in any scenario, both real and imagined. Yet when the perpetrators are state actors victimizing the citizenry, blatant lawlessness is routinely ignored. Their refusal to protect the public from the threat of lawless policing is a direct factor in the escalation of police criminality and violence. Without meaningful accountability imposed by the federal government, unlawful police violence is certain to continue and intensify.

"*[Attorney General Eric] Holder . . . has
demonstrated no reluctance to place the
power of the federal government behind probes into police misconduct.*"

The Federal Government Is Enthusiastically Combating Police Brutality

Jessica Wehrman and Jack Torry

*In the following viewpoint, Jessica Wehrman and Jack Torry ar-
gue that the US federal government is doing its utmost to investigate and eliminate police brutality. Attorney General Eric
Holder, they write, is highly interested in examining the ways
that police interact with minorities. This is because President
Barack Obama is fully devoted to making police practices everywhere equal and safe. Wehrman and Torry are writers for the*
Columbus Dispatch *in central Ohio.*

As you read, consider the following questions:

1. According to the authors' research, what is the current
   status of minorities' relationship with police departments in the United States?

2. According to the authors, why has Holder's investigation into police misconduct upset some conservative politicians?

3. According to the authors' research, why is it difficult to prosecute a police officer under federal law?

The Justice Department's decision to investigate the shooting death last month [August 2014] of a Fairfield, Ohio, man by police is part of an aggressive effort nationwide by outgoing attorney general Eric Holder to scrutinize what he has described as "police misconduct."

During his 5½ years as attorney general, Holder has launched more than twice as many civil rights investigations into potential police misconduct as any other attorney general.

Just last week, Carter M. Stewart, the U.S. attorney for the southern district of Ohio, announced his office will investigate whether police violated the civil rights of John Crawford III when they shot him to death in a Walmart store in Beavercreek, near Dayton. Stewart made the announcement the same day a special grand jury in Ohio decided to not indict the police officers.

In a higher-profile case, the Justice Department launched a probe after police fatally shot Michael Brown, who was black and unarmed, in Ferguson, Mo., last month. That shooting sparked nights of angry demonstrations in the St. Louis suburb.

And in 2012, Holder ordered Justice Department officials to determine whether George Zimmerman, who had been serving as a neighborhood watch officer in Sanford, Fla., violated the civil rights of Trayvon Martin when he shot and killed the black 17-year-old.

No Federal Reluctance

Although it is extremely difficult to prosecute a police officer in a civil rights case, Holder—the nation's first African American attorney general and who announced last week he will leave his post as soon as a successor has been confirmed—has demonstrated no reluctance to place the power of the federal government behind probes into police misconduct.

"Two things are driving the attorney general to be more aggressive than his predecessors," said Ronald Sullivan, a professor at Harvard Law School. "One is the attorney general deeply believes in the concept of equal justice under the law and in viewing the way many minority citizens experience the justice system, that is not a reality.

"The second reason is the attorney general sees growing discomfort among large segments of the citizenry with the police," said Sullivan, who in 2008 chaired a criminal-justice policy committee for the presidential campaign of Barack Obama. "That is to say the relationship between minorities and police departments is as bad as it has been for the past 40 to 50 years."

In a speech last week before the Brennan Center for Justice at the New York University School of Law, Holder said, "It's time to ask ourselves—as a nation—are we conducting policing in the 21st century in a manner that is as effective, as efficient, and as equitable and as just as is possible?"

Holder said, "as an African American man—who has been stopped and searched by police in situations where such action was not warranted—I also carry with me an understanding of the mistrust that some citizens harbor for those who wear the badge."

To Holder's defenders, he has focused on one of the country's most divisive issues. Rep. Joyce Beatty, D-Jefferson Township [Ohio], said, "Beavercreek is like a Ferguson in many ways."

"I think it tells us that we have to do a better job of educating on both sides for the safety of all, for our police officers and the safety for our communities," she said.

Sen. Sherrod Brown, D-Ohio, who backed the Justice Department's decision to examine the Beavercreek shooting, said Stewart "has a different set of criteria and the U.S. attorney looks at this from a civil rights viewpoint. Sometimes looking at this from a little further away can be a little more accurate gauge."

Holder's actions have left some conservatives queasy. Rep. Jim Jordan, R-Urbana [Ohio], said, "My attitude is let's let the normal criminal-justice process work. That is a locally and state-driven process."

But acknowledging that Ohio attorney general Mike De-Wine and Gov. John Kasich support the Justice Department probe, Jordan said he was "fine with it as well. I have a great deal of respect for . . . Mike DeWine, and if he thinks this is appropriate, fine."

In an interview with the *Dayton Daily News*, Stewart said, "The first step will be reviewing what the state did and making a determination if we need to do that. That could entail reinterviewing witnesses that have already been interviewed or interviewing people who have not been interviewed."

While declining to say how long the review will take, Stewart said, "We will receive all of the evidence they had in this case, as well as grand jury testimony. We will do our own independent analysis . . . to determine whether there is a case to proceed on as well."

Vigorous Legal Pursuit

Legal analysts say, however, it is extremely difficult to prosecute police officers under federal law. Thaddeus Hoffmeister, a law professor at the University of Dayton, said, "The problem is you have to show the specific intent of the police officer."

He added that it would be difficult to demonstrate that the police entered the Walmart store "with the idea" that they planned to violate Crawford's constitutional rights.

But federal probes can prompt changes by local police. In July, the Justice Department and the city of Albuquerque, N.M., reached agreement on a wide range of reforms to be implemented by the city's police department.

In April, the Justice Department had charged that the police department "engages in a pattern or practice of use of excessive force, including deadly force, in violation of" federal law and the U.S. Constitution.

Sullivan said, "Even if it does not lead to a prosecution or a lawsuit, it provides space for local self-reflection."

Local officials will "take a good, hard look at their police practices," he said.

"I am confident the next attorney general will pursue (these cases) just as vigorously" as Holder has, Sullivan said. "This is a priority of the president."

> *"It was left to none other than President Obama to remind Americans that police brutality is an issue that impacts everyone and should not be about race."*

Obama Is Correct to Separate Police Brutality from Racism

Paul Joseph Watson

In the following viewpoint, Paul Joseph Watson commends President Barack Obama for distinguishing between police brutality and racism. Watson writes that both police violence and the proliferation of crime among certain communities are mostly to blame for American deaths by police. Watson believes the justice system for abusive police must be reformed for brutality to be stopped. Watson is editor at large of Infowars.com.

As you read, consider the following questions:

1. How does Watson say white Americans have attempted to rectify what is perceived as their "white privilege" with police?

2. How does Watson say the Ferguson, Missouri, protests against police are ineffective?

3. What does Watson say are the statistics regarding African American homicides as they relate to the African American population?

They say a broken clock is right twice a day and that old adage proved true last night [in December 2014] when President [Barack] Obama made the point that the proper response to the Eric Garner controversy should be to focus on police brutality, not race.

Protesters flooded the streets of New York last night after a grand jury decided not to charge Officer Daniel Pantaleo in the death of 43-year-old Eric Garner, who was choked to death for the crime of selling untaxed cigarettes. Video footage of the incident clearly shows that Garner offered little or no resistance and was not acting aggressively toward officers during the arrest.

Despite an army of social justice warriors immediately reacting to the decision by stoking yet more racial division, it was left to none other than President Obama to remind Americans that police brutality is an issue that impacts everyone and should not be about race.

"It is incumbent on all of us as Americans, regardless of race, region, faith, that we recognize this is an American problem, not just a black problem, or a brown problem, or a Native American problem. This is an American problem," said Obama during a Tribal Nations conference at the White House.

The Real Problem

Unfortunately, Obama's sober analysis was almost universally ignored by irate leftists, who took to Twitter to blame Garner's death on white people rather than corrupt police officers.

Is Police Brutality Color-Blind?

A survey released this week [in August 2014] by the Pew Research Center has revealed glaring differences of views among blacks and whites when it comes to the death of Michael Brown, an unarmed African American youth killed by a white police officer in Ferguson, Missouri, on Aug. 9, and the protests that have followed.

Unfortunately though, the wording of the survey leaves some pertinent questions unaddressed, focusing on the racial aspect of the controversy while overlooking the public's general perception about the problem of police brutality in America.

Nevertheless, the survey significantly found that blacks are about twice as likely as whites to say that Brown's shooting "raises important issues about race that need to be discussed," with about 80 percent of African Americans agreeing with that statement and whites saying by a 47 percent . . . margin that the issue of race is getting more attention than it deserves.

Although the Pew survey neglected to ask, it's possible that at least some of the white respondents objected to the focus on race because they feel that the epidemic of police violence cuts across racial lines. As anyone who regularly follows news pertaining to police brutality knows, the police are generally out of control across the country and the victims of their brutishness are not just African Americans—but in fact, Latinos, Asians, and yes, even white people.

Nat Parry,
"Is Police Brutality Color-Blind?,"
Consortiumnews.com, August 22, 2014.

By the evening, the hashtag #CrimingWhileWhite was trending and Caucasians were falling over themselves to apologize for their "white privilege" by telling anecdotal tales of how they had escaped police retribution after committing minor offenses.

Absent from the discussion was the fact that "white privilege" counted for very little in the cases of both Kelly Thomas and James Boyd, both white, both homeless, both of whom were summarily executed by police officers as they begged for their lives—just like Eric Garner.

Instead of what should have happened—conservatives and liberals, blacks and whites unifying against police brutality—the left has managed to turn the Ferguson protests and the Eric Garner backlash into Occupy 2.0—a divisive faux "revolution" which will go nowhere because it alienates half the population of the United States.

Instead of having a nuanced debate about what drives police profiling of black people and why cops immediately resort to violence in many cases, collectivists have ensured that the narrative is focused solely on "white guilt," a misdirection that only serves to fuel a cultural race war, while communist groups have also hijacked the cause to push anticapitalist economic sectarianism.

FBI [Federal Bureau of Investigation] crime statistics show that black people commit almost the same number of homicides as whites and Hispanics put together, yet they represent only 13 percent of the population. Again, despite representing only a fraction of the population, 93 percent of blacks are killed by other blacks, according to Justice Department figures.

This problem of criminality and violence in the black community has nothing to do with skin color and everything to do with the glamorized 'thug life' culture promoted by (white-owned) entertainment companies via hip-hop and rap music.

The problem of brutality and abuse of force among police officers has nothing to do with skin color and everything to do with increased militarization and federal training which encourages cops to see citizens as the enemy in a war zone.

Both of these integral factors have received little or no attention as a result of social justice vultures making the issue all about race. This isn't about "white privilege," it's about "blue privilege," a system that allows cops to get away with murder no matter the skin color of the victim.

This misplaced anger can only please the establishment, since it ensures that everyone is kept locked into a futile furor of blaming each other while the true causes of police brutality directed toward both the black community and the wider population remain unaddressed.

> "When the police and other state-sanctioned vigilantes are killing African Americans at a rate of one every 28 hours, people won't accept toothless reforms."

Obama Is Wrong to Separate Police Brutality from Racism

Keeanga-Yamahtta Taylor

In the following viewpoint, Keeanga-Yamahtta Taylor argues that racism is an inherent component of police brutality. Blacks are targeted for arrests and police abuse more than whites are, she asserts, perpetuating a careless attitude among police for black lives. Police officers must be held accountable for their actions, Taylor believes, so black communities can stop being torn apart by law enforcement. Taylor is an assistant professor at Princeton University's Center for African American Studies.

As you read, consider the following questions:

1. What phrases does Taylor want the federal government to invoke with regard to police brutality?

2. What does Taylor say was a major problem for blacks under the Bill Clinton administration?

3. How much does Taylor say Philadelphia has paid for complaints against police from 2008 to 2014?

Less than a month before Mike Brown [a young African American man shot and killed by a police officer in Ferguson, Missouri] became an international symbol of police violence and racism in American law enforcement, Eric Garner was choked to death in broad daylight on a sidewalk on Staten Island in New York City. As Officer Daniel Pantaleo literally squeezed the life out of him, Garner repeated 11 times, "I can't breathe."

The killings may have taken place half a continent apart and the causes of death were different, but Brown and Garner will be forever linked in people's minds because grand juries in the two cases decided, within days of each other, not to indict a white police officer who killed an unarmed African American man.

In Brown's case, several witnesses testified that Brown's hands were raised in the surrender position when Officer Darren Wilson continued to shoot, ultimately killing Brown in a hail of bullets.

In Garner's case, there were witnesses, too—but the whole world could watch his murder unfold on a video recording. The Garner case evoked memories of the video recording of the beating of Rodney King [a man beaten by Los Angeles police officers in 1991]. The outcome was the same—black America reacted with disbelief as the four white officers who almost killed King were exonerated, despite the video evidence of their brutality against an unarmed man.

With Garner, as with the case of Mike Brown, two grand juries came to the same conclusion: no probable cause to go forward with a trial. The message could not be any clearer that in the eyes of the law, and especially law enforcement, black men and women have no rights that officers are bound to respect.

Broken Windows

The impact of these cases, coming within days of each other, produced a genuine crisis in American policing, and its defenders are scrambling to hold onto whatever fraying threads of legitimacy remain.

In response to the resurgent wave of protests in Ferguson after the grand jury announcement, there was an unprecedented meeting that brought grassroots anti–police brutality activists into the same room with President Barack Obama, Vice President Joe Biden and Attorney General Eric Holder. Out of this and other discussions, Obama emerged with a proposal he hopes will restore confidence in law enforcement, including a pilot program for 50,000 police to wear body cameras, a review of how local police departments utilize military equipment, and a new commission to study policing and community relations.

The announcement from the White House barely had time to make a ripple before the non-indictment of Eric Garner's killer reduced the plan to a pile of junk. In one stroke, the idea that body cameras could make a difference in whether a police officer would be held responsible for the death of an innocent and unarmed person collapsed—and with it, the centerpiece of Obama's proposed reforms.

The focus on body cameras assumes that the reason violent and brutal police aren't punished is because of the absence of visual evidence or proof. But this has nothing to do with it, as the Eric Garner case makes crystal clear. Instead, violence in American policing goes unpunished because the criminalization of black people has legitimized brutality, humiliation, incarceration and even murder as reasonable practices.

That Obama and Holder have launched initiatives to address policing in black communities, and yet phrases like "racial inequality," "mass incarceration" and "racial profiling" are never invoked, raises questions as to whether this is a serious inquiry or a stalling mechanism designed to give the impression that action is being taken, when in reality, they are simply buying time in the hopes that black Americans will cool off.

In fact, it is impossible to imagine any serious response to police brutality in black communities not involving the undoing of the so-called "war on drugs" and all of the resulting effects of mass incarceration.

The cumulative impact of these policies has cemented the public perception that all working-class African American men and women are suspicious and worthy of close scrutiny and surveillance. Police transform these perceptions into policy, as black communities are targeted and suffer overwhelmingly disproportionate rates of "stops and frisks," frivolous arrests and other engagement that can only be described as harassment.

This is the essence of the "broken windows" theory of policing—first pioneered in New York City during the first reign of current police chief William Bratton, but now practiced across the country.

The "theory" is that if low-level offenses are aggressively policed, more serious offenses will be deterred. In reality, this approach to policing has criminalized entire communities, leading to thousands of frivolous arrests that ruin people's lives.

Moreover, policing in the neoliberal era relies on all sorts of statistics that document the rise and fall of crime and incentivize the manipulation of numbers to shape the perception of crime-fighting in a given locality. Politicians regularly invoke arrest numbers, crime rates (when they're going down) and other supposed markers of "crime-fighting" as evidence of their competence—big-city police chiefs parlay these statistics into pay raises and political capital. They are all getting fat off the destruction of the lives of the young black men and women who are the overwhelming victims of American policing and unjust practices in the wider judicial system.

Foxes and Chickens

None of the reforms that Obama and Holder at the federal level or New York City mayor Bill de Blasio are suggesting will do anything to address these systemic issues. Instead, Obama's commission on policing in the 21st century is likely to produce many of the same "reforms" that created the problems in the first place.

The commission is to be led by former assistant attorney general Laurie Robinson and Philadelphia police chief Charles Ramsey. These two particular people at the helm of a commission aimed at curbing errant police conduct in black communities is akin to putting the fox in charge of investigating a rash of attacks on chickens. It's literally absurd.

All one needs to know about Robinson is that she worked in the Department of Justice for seven years during the [Bill] Clinton administration, when the U.S. became known as the "incarceration nation." Under Clinton, the federal and state prison populations rose faster than under any other administration in American history—the rate at which black people were incarcerated tripled.

As an assistant attorney general, Robinson will have had her fingerprints all over Clinton's signature crime legislation, which included the immoral and racist expansion of the use of the death penalty, as well as adopting the "three strikes and you're out" sentencing rule that helped to explode the prison population across the nation.

As for Ramsey, the idea that *any* law enforcement official from Philadelphia could have any meaningful contribution to the national discussion on curbing police brutality and racism in black communities is an affront to common sense.

Philadelphia is, of course, home to a police union that remains committed to using its resources to keep black political prisoner Mumia Abu-Jamal [convicted in the shooting death of a Philadelphia police officer in 1981] behind bars. It is also where the police participated in the bombing of MOVE activists, a black counterculture organization, in the 1980s.

Aside from these spectacular examples of police misconduct and racism, there is the daily targeting of black communities, which has, to take just one example, led to disproportionate rates of arrest and imprisonment for nonviolent drug offenses. Despite the fact that blacks and whites use marijuana at relatively the same rate, blacks were four times more likely to be arrested and charged with possession. According to one study, of the adults arrested in 2012 for marijuana possession, 3,052 were black compared to 629 whites.

What is Charles Ramsey's role in this? Even though the Philadelphia City Council voted to ease laws criminalizing pot possession, Ramsey spent last summer insisting that his police department would continue to arrest people for possession. His public statement: "I am not in favor at all of any form of [marijuana] legalization. . . . We still have to treat [marijuana possession] as a misdemeanor until we are told otherwise by state law. . . . State law trumps city ordinances."

Finally, since Ramsey became chief of police in 2008, the city of Philadelphia has paid out $40 million to settle lawsuits involving wrongful shooting deaths, illegal searches or excessive force complaints.

Just last May, Philadelphia was forced to pay $14 million to settle a civil rights lawsuit against police that involved 128 plaintiffs. In 2012, the city negotiated deals on several different cases of police misconduct, at a cost of $8 million. As one lawyer who successfully sued the city explained about Philly police, "The rank and file have no expectation that their be-

United Nations Questions United States on Use of Force

The United States has mounted a vigorous defense of Washington's pursuit of justice for all its citizens at a United Nations public hearing to examine the U.S.'s human rights record. . . .

The U.S. was represented at the hearing by a large legal team fielding questions and sharp criticism from U.N. member states about the U.S. human rights record. The most persistent observations and expressions of disapproval had to do with alleged discriminatory practices against racial minorities and the excessive use of force by law enforcement.

The U.S. delegation said it was proud of the country's human rights record, but admitted the record was not spotless. It fell to James Cadogan, senior counselor to the assistant attorney general in the U.S. Department of Justice, to explain several controversial cases involving police and minorities, including the fatal shooting last year of 18-year-old Michael Brown in Ferguson, Missouri. The police officer who shot and killed the African American teenager was not indicted. . . .

Countries participating in the debate proposed a number of recommendations to the U.S. These included calls for the U.S. to abolish capital punishment, close the Guantánamo Bay detention facility, prevent acts of torture, eliminate racial discrimination in all its forms and combat violence against women.

Lisa Schlein,
"UN Grills US on Police Brutality, Racial Bias,"
Voice of America, May 11, 2015.

havior is ever going to be subject to any real, meaningful review.... That becomes admissible evidence that shows the city is not properly supervising and disciplining officers."

What on earth does the Philadelphia Police Department have to teach the nation about ending racism and brutality in American policing?

Toothless Reforms

This is a crisis that won't go away. As the U.S. continues to assert its authority internationally, the ugly fact of white police officers murdering and abusing black men and women looms over American actions abroad. It renders hollow the kind of rhetoric that Barack Obama employed when he framed the new U.S. war on ISIS [also known as ISIL, the Islamic State of Iraq and the Levant, or the Islamic State] back in September, saying:

> [O]ur endless blessings bestow an enduring burden. But as Americans, we welcome our responsibility to lead. From Europe to Asia, from the far reaches of Africa to war-torn capitals of the Middle East, we stand for freedom, for justice, for dignity. These are values that have guided our nation since its founding.

These comments didn't fit reality then, but today, they are completely absurd. The U.S. has not an ounce of credibility when it comes to any discussion about freedom, justice and dignity.

At home, Obama has directly inserted himself into this crisis, and in doing so, he is raising the expectations of African Americans that he will finally use his office to do something other than chastise black people. Talking about the Eric Garner case, Obama said, "We are going to take specific steps to improve the training and the work with state and local government when it comes to policing in communities of color. . . . We are going to be scrupulous in investigating cases where we are concerned about the partiality and accountability that's taking place."

But the question remains how, when all the parties involved refuse to address the systemic issues involving criminalization, racial profiling and mass incarceration. How many more commissions and investigations are needed to come to the obvious conclusion that the police operate above the law, and that legal institutions generally view black people, especially black men, as expendable?

When the police and other state-sanctioned vigilantes are killing African Americans at a rate of one every 28 hours, people won't accept toothless reforms meant to quell anger while doing absolutely nothing to punish, imprison and disarm the real menace—the agents of the state who terrorize African American communities with impunity.

> *"Ultimately, it is unrealistic for us to expect the federal government to swoop in and provide justice in individual cases."*

The Department of Justice Cannot Correct All Police Brutality

Imani Gandy

In the following viewpoint, Imani Gandy argues that the US Department of Justice cannot be relied upon to root out and punish all incidents of police brutality around the country. This is because it is difficult for federal prosecutors to overcome the legal difficulties of indicting individual officers. Rather, Gandy believes, the government is better at finding and reforming patterns of misconduct in police forces. Gandy is senior legal analyst at RH Reality Check.

As you read, consider the following questions:

1. What does Gandy say is a major obstacle to federal prosecution of police officers?

2. What legal action does Gandy say the Justice Department will take against the city of Cleveland for police misconduct?

3. How does Gandy say the prosecution of individual police officers can lead to police complacency?

Last week [in December 2014], following the announcement that the New York grand jury had decided not to indict Daniel Pantaleo in the killing of Eric Garner, Eric Holder announced that the Department of Justice [DOJ] would be opening an investigation into the matter. And the Monday prior, after the no-indictment decision by the grand jury in Ferguson [Missouri], the DOJ reassured us that the investigation into Darren Wilson that they had begun back in August immediately after Mike Brown's death would continue.

We often greet such announcements with cheers and open arms. And indeed, a DOJ investigation may lead to much-needed structural reforms of the police departments under scrutiny. But for those of us who want justice for Eric Garner and Mike Brown *specifically*, the truth of the matter is that the DOJ doesn't have a lot of options.

Pattern or Practice

As mentioned previously by Jessica Mason Pieklo on *RH Reality Check*, the DOJ could bring a lawsuit against the police officers under 18 U.S. Code section 242, a federal statute that authorizes the prosecution of police officers for violation of citizens' constitutional rights. In addition to the problems Pieklo discussed that can arise from federal prosecutors coordinating with local police forces, the burden of proof for such cases is practically insurmountable: The prosecutor has to prove that the police officer *willfully* subjected a person to the deprivation of his or her constitutional rights.

In other words, a federal prosecutor would have to prove that not only did Darren Wilson and Daniel Pantaleo use excessive force against Mike Brown and Eric Garner respectively, but also that they *intended* to do so. And as you might imagine, it's very difficult to prove intent at trial unless there is video evidence of an egregious violation of constitutional rights, as there was with the eventual successful federal prosecution of two of the four [Los Angeles] police officers who assaulted Rodney King [in 1991].

But, you may be thinking, there's video evidence in the Eric Garner case—isn't that enough?

Maybe. The fact that Pantaleo used a banned technique to subdue Eric Garner—the choke hold that ultimately led to Garner's death—certainly helps. But it's likely that a federal grand jury wouldn't find that constitutes sufficient probable cause to believe that Pantaleo *willfully* violated Garner's constitutional rights. And it's even more likely that a federal prosecutor would find it impossible to prove that Pantaleo *intended* to kill Garner. A federal jury would likely decide that Garner's death was an accident. I think it's safe to say that Pantaleo's actions don't rise to the same level of egregiousness as a police officer beating Rodney King into a pulp at the behest of his police sergeant.

The fact of the matter is that the DOJ is better at dealing with structural problems in a particular police department through "pattern or practice" cases than it is at prosecuting individual police officers for instances of excessive force or police brutality.

Pattern or practice cases are brought by the Department of Justice under the Violent Crime Control and Law Enforcement Act, which Congress passed in the wake of the Rodney King beating and the subsequent riots. The law authorizes the U.S. attorney general to file lawsuits against entire police departments that have engaged in a "pattern or practice" of violating citizens' civil rights in order to force them to reform.

For example, just last week, the DOJ released a "pattern or practice" report containing the results of its investigation into the Cleveland Police Department, which it began in March 2013. (That police department currently happens to be in hot water because one of its officers essentially executed 12-year-old Tamir Rice in what journalist Ta-Nehisi Coates aptly described as a "state-authorized drive-by.")

As a result, Cleveland, under threat of being sued for civil rights violations by the DOJ, will be forced into a consent decree, which is a settlement agreement authorized by a federal judge, between the police department and the federal government. Based on the requirements of previous consent decrees, this will likely require Cleveland to implement reforms such as mandating cultural sensitivity training for police officers, creating new "use of force" policies, keeping automated records on the performance of police officers, enacting early warning systems to identify problem officers, increasing community outreach, and the like. Once the attorney general is satisfied that Cleveland has complied with the terms of the consent decree, the federal judge overseeing the case will release Cleveland from its obligations under it.

Most consent decrees last for a period of five years, but some reform efforts can take a decade or more. For example, the consent decree imposed on the LAPD [Los Angeles Police Department] in 2001 in the wake of the Rampart Division scandal [involving corruption among officers in the division] was just lifted last year. And of course, if at some point in the future Cleveland regresses and there are more rights violations, then the federal government can open a new investigation and subject Cleveland to yet another consent decree. (The Pittsburgh Police Department, for example, is currently under investigation for corruption and may be subject to another consent decree barely a decade after the first consent decree was lifted.)

Forced to Reform

Since cop culture is generally resistant to change, these sorts of consent decrees are important tools that compel police departments to examine the way they have been operating and to reform their practices in order to better serve the communities they police. And, in a sense, they are more useful than the prosecutions of individual police officers, since consent decrees require structural and meaningful change in the ways that police departments operate. In turn, these sorts of reforms can reduce incidents of police misconduct and senseless brutality. While prosecutions of individual police officers may be satisfying, they can lead to complacency in police departments, which may be quick to dismiss an individual case as the rogue actions of one bad apple.

I don't mean to suggest that the DOJ never prosecutes individual police officers. They do. The Rodney King trial is a shining example of that. But the Rodney King trial involved a group of police officers practically beating a man to death in a manner that could never be construed as "accidental" or "unintentional." In general, however, the burden of proof in federal police misconduct cases is so high that winning such a case is nearly impossible—and it's therefore unlikely a prosecutor would take it on.

Ultimately, it is unrealistic for us to expect the federal government to swoop in and provide justice in individual cases, especially when the tools that they have at their disposal are limited. I hate to be a downer, but we need to be realistic about the sort of justice we can expect from federal prosecutors after state prosecutors refuse to file charges or secure grand jury indictments.

The bottom line is this: It's unlikely Wilson or Pantaleo will be prosecuted. It's far more likely that the Ferguson and New York City Police Departments will be forced to reform.

And while that is cold comfort to the families of Mike Brown and Eric Garner, the sort of reform that results from consent decrees just might decrease tensions between the police and the communities they are supposed to serve.

> *"Congress passed the Violent Crime Control and Law Enforcement Act, which included a provision that gave the Justice Department unprecedented power to investigate law enforcement agencies for systemic problems."*

The Department of Justice Can Help Correct Police Brutality

Sarah Childress

In the following viewpoint, Sarah Childress contends that the US Department of Justice has been resolutely working to combat police brutality in America. Its investigations into the wrongful practices of police departments in the past, Childress writes, have led to reformed policing tactics. The department must continue these efforts, Childress believes, so that America's police can be truly reformed and serve their communities more effectively. Childress is a writer for PBS's news series Frontline.

As you read, consider the following questions:

1. What does Childress's research say is usually a necessary component of police reform?

2. What does Childress say was the cost and length of time it took for the Justice Department to investigate Los Angeles police, signaling a flawed reform process?

3. What did the Justice Department discover about Newark, New Jersey, police in 2014?

Ferguson, Mo., police officers regularly discriminate against black residents, subjecting them to illegal stops, excessive force and arrests for petty offenses like "manner of walking in roadway," according to a Department of Justice (DOJ) investigation released on Wednesday [in March 2015].

The DOJ opened a probe into the department in September 2014, one month after police officer Darren Wilson shot and killed Michael Brown, an unarmed black 18-year-old. No criminal charges were brought against the officer, who has resigned from the department. A civil rights investigation into Wilson yielded no charges, the DOJ said Wednesday.

The broader DOJ investigation examined whether the Ferguson Police Department [FPD] fostered a culture of bias against African Americans that could have contributed to the circumstances surrounding Brown's death.

"Of course, violence is never justified," Attorney General Eric Holder said at a press conference following the report's release. "But seen in this context—amid a highly toxic environment, defined by mistrust and resentment, stoked by years of bad feelings, and spurred by illegal and misguided practices—it is not difficult to imagine how a single tragic incident set off the city of Ferguson like a powder keg."

The investigation also began amid nationwide protests that erupted over a series of police killings of unarmed black males last year, including Eric Garner, who was choked to death by a

New York (NYPD) police officer in July; John Crawford III, gunned down by police in an Ohio Walmart in August; Brown, who was killed a few days later; Akai Gurley, shot to death in a housing project stairwell on Nov. 20 by a NYPD officer; and Tamir Rice, a 12-year-old boy shot dead in a park by Cleveland police on Nov. 22. Rice had been holding a toy gun.

Their deaths have led to widespread calls for police reform and brought to the surface long-standing sentiments in the African American community that they are treated with more suspicion and hostility by police.

Policing the Police

The investigation of the Ferguson Police Department is one outcome of a federal law, passed in the wake of a notorious incident of police violence: the 1991 case of Rodney King, a black man who was beaten by Los Angeles police after being stopped for speeding. Three years later, Congress passed the Violent Crime Control and Law Enforcement Act, which included a provision that gave the Justice Department unprecedented power to investigate law enforcement agencies for systemic problems—such as use of excessive force, or racial profiling—and force them to implement reforms.

The law is the only tool that exists to compel widespread change within a police department. The Justice Department can threaten to sue a department for constitutional violations, forcing it to enter into a negotiated settlement, such as a consent decree.

"It's often hard to reform police departments without external intervention," said Erwin Chemerinsky, dean of the University of California, Irvine law school, and an expert on constitutional policing. "Institutions are resistant to change. None of us like to have somebody outside telling us what to do. And police departments are especially that way. They have their own internal culture."

In the past 20 years, the Justice Department has launched at least 65 so-called "pattern or practice" investigations of law enforcement agencies, 32 of which have led to agreements to reform, according to an analysis of DOJ data by Stephen Rushin, a professor at the University of Illinois [College of Law] who studies police misconduct.

That's a small number compared to the nearly 18,000 law enforcement agencies nationwide.

Still, the reforms have had an impact: Today, nearly one in five Americans is served by a law enforcement agency that has been subject to a DOJ investigation under this law, according to Rushin's analysis.

Most investigations zero in on whether, when and how officers are allowed to use force, including deadly force. Also atop the list: a focus on discriminatory policing of minorities—specifically, blacks and Latinos. The DOJ has also examined allegations of gender discrimination, the treatment of people in the LGBT [lesbian, gay, bisexual, and transgender] community, and how officers handle people who are mentally ill.

A New Push for Civil Rights Investigations

The [Barack] Obama administration has used its power aggressively to take on widespread problems of police brutality, discrimination and other abuse in local jurisdictions, negotiating more settlement agreements than either the [Bill] Clinton or George W. Bush administrations.

"In case you haven't heard, the Civil Rights Division is once again open for business," said Thomas Perez, the assistant attorney general tapped to lead the division, in a 2010 speech. Combating police misconduct, he said, had become an important priority—and pattern or practice investigations were a "critical tool" for bringing change.

Under Attorney General Eric Holder, the Justice Department has opened 20 investigations and negotiated agreements to implement reforms in 15 departments, including major cities like New Orleans, La., Portland, Ore., and Newark, N.J. It currently has nine open investigations.

Even the Justice Department admits flaws in the process. It's expensive and can take years to fulfill an agreement. In Los Angeles, which is widely considered the most successful test case, it took more than a decade for the police to complete the required reforms, at a cost of $15 million. And the DOJ's process for choosing departments to investigate, often sparked by a combination of news reports and complaints from local civil rights groups or public officials, can make the law feel haphazardly applied.

The DOJ assessed its process in 2010, noting that some police chiefs said that federal investigations create a negative stigma that's difficult to dispel. They urged a more collaborative approach.

But in some departments, it may be the only way to bring about significant change. Charles Ramsey was the chief of the Metropolitan Police Department in Washington, D.C., when he asked the Justice Department to investigate in 1999, following a series of stories in the *Washington Post* that said that the department killed more residents per capita than police in any other major city. The resulting agreement led to major reforms, significantly reducing the number of police shootings and boosting the department's credibility in the community, Ramsey said.

"We would not have been able to make the changes we made without the consent decree," he said at a 2013 conference. "We would have encountered push back from the union, and we would not have obtained the funding."

What the Justice Department Found in Ferguson

In its Ferguson investigation, the DOJ was looking for a pattern or practice of discriminatory policing and examining the department's use of force.

What it found included routine violations of black residents' civil rights. For example, the DOJ found that black drivers were more than twice as likely as white drivers to be searched during traffic stops, but 26 percent less likely to be found with contraband. Even so, black drivers were more likely to be cited and arrested during a traffic stop.

The report also found that 88 percent of documented police use-of-force cases involved blacks, and in particular juveniles and people with mental health problems or cognitive disabilities.

Some petty offenses appear to be reserved largely for African Americans. From 2011 to 2013, a full 95 percent of people charged with a crime called "manner of walking in roadway" were black, as were 94 percent of those charged with "failure to comply."

"Many FPD uses of force appear entirely punitive," the report concluded.

The city used these kinds of citations to generate revenue, the DOJ found. In 2015, the city anticipated raising more than $3 million in fines and fees—more than double the total from five years earlier.

"Many officers appear to see some residents, especially those who live in Ferguson's predominantly African American neighborhoods, less as constituents to be protected than as potential offenders and sources of revenue," the report said.

Next Steps for Ferguson

The Justice Department made 26 recommendations for reform in Ferguson and will insist on a court-enforced agreement to make those changes. The next step for Ferguson will be to decide whether to negotiate or fight federal officials in court. That process can take months, or even years.

Some departments, like Newark, have cooperated with federal authorities. In July 2014, the Justice Department found that Newark police had a pattern or practice of dispropor-

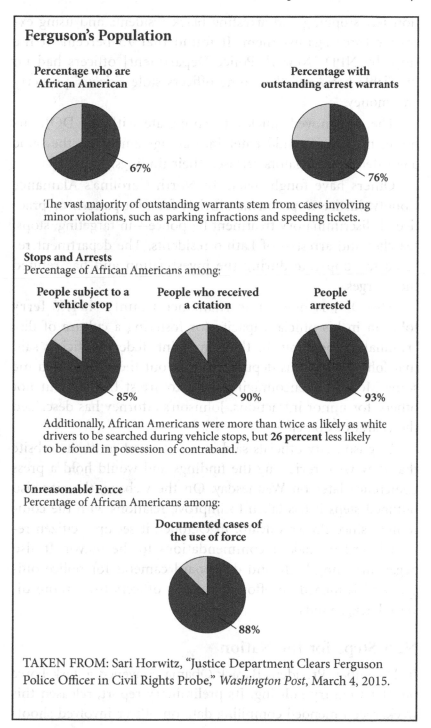

Ferguson's Population

Percentage who are African American

67%

Percentage with outstanding arrest warrants

76%

The vast majority of outstanding warrants stem from cases involving minor violations, such as parking infractions and speeding tickets.

Stops and Arrests
Percentage of African Americans among:

People subject to a vehicle stop

85%

People who received a citation

90%

People arrested

93%

Additionally, African Americans were more than twice as likely as white drivers to be searched during vehicle stops, but **26 percent** less likely to be found in possession of contraband.

Unreasonable Force
Percentage of African Americans among:

Documented cases of the use of force

88%

TAKEN FROM: Sari Horwitz, "Justice Department Clears Ferguson Police Officer in Civil Rights Probe," *Washington Post*, March 4, 2015.

tionately stopping and arresting black residents and using excessive force against them. It found that 75 percent of the stops by NPD [Newark Police Department] officers had no justifiable basis and that some officers stole citizens' property and money.

The city moved quickly to cooperate with the DOJ, announcing that it would enter into an agreement on the same day federal investigators released their findings.

Others have fought back. In North Carolina's Alamance County, Justice Department officials found a pattern or practice of discriminatory treatment by police—in targeting, stops, searches and arrests—of Latino residents. The department refused to cooperate during the investigation and has refuted the charges.

The DOJ is now suing Alamance County sheriff Terry Johnson in his official capacity for fostering a culture of discriminatory policing. In the complaint, federal officials said that Johnson told his deputies to "Go out there and catch me some Mexicans," encouraging them to arrest Latinos, but not others, for minor infractions. Johnson's attorney has described the charges as baseless.

Ferguson city officials said in a statement on their website that they were reviewing the findings and would hold a press conference later on Wednesday. On the website, the city also outlined steps it has taken to improve relations with the community since Brown's death. In October, it set up a citizen review board to make recommendations to the mayor. It also began installing body and dashboard cameras for police officers and launched an effort to recruit officers from more diverse backgrounds.

Next Steps for the Nation

In December, President Barack Obama convened a Task Force on 21st Century Policing. Its preliminary report, released this week, recommended compiling data on officer-involved shootings and establishing independent investigations of such incidents. It also recommended reducing police use of military equipment during protests, though it stopped short of recommending the widespread use of body cameras for officers, citing privacy concerns.

The task force also recommended that departments work to build trust in communities of color. A survey it conducted found that 72 percent of whites said they were confident officers would treat people of other races the same way; only 46 percent of Hispanics and 36 percent of blacks agreed.

Periodical and Internet Sources Bibliography

The following articles have been selected to supplement the diverse views presented in this chapter.

Luke Broadwater and Mark Puente	"Federal Review of Baltimore Police Brutality to Be 'Candid,' Official Says," *Baltimore Sun*, October 8, 2014.
Jamil Dakwar	"How Does the Federal Government Handle Prosecutions of Police Officers?," American Civil Liberties Union, February 24, 2015.
Lauren Fox	"Is Congress Powerless to Combat Police Brutality?," *National Journal*, April 28, 2015.
Ben Mathis-Lilley	"Obama Calls Police Violence a 'Crisis,' Condemns Mass Neglect of Poor," *Slate*, April 28, 2015.
Ian Millhiser	"Justice Department Uncovers Absurd Levels of Police Brutality in the Cleveland Police Force," *ThinkProgress*, December 5, 2014.
Jamil Smith	"You, Too, Can Prevent Police Brutality," *New Republic*, March 4, 2015.
Phillip Swarts	"Police Need Better Training and Community Relations, Presidential Task Force Is Told," *Washington Times*, January 13, 2015.
Alex S. Vitale	"Obama's Police Reforms Ignore the Most Important Cause of Police Misconduct," *Nation*, March 6, 2015.
Taylor Wofford	"15 Most Outrageous Examples of Police Misconduct in the DOJ Report on Ferguson," *Newsweek*, March 4, 2015.

For Further Discussion

Chapter 1

1. Richard Rowe identifies a number of steps that he believes would end police brutality in the United States, such as requiring officers to wear multiple body cameras and eliminating officers' "trained observer" status. Do you think the steps Rowe identifies would eliminate police brutality in America? Why, or why not? Do you think any of the steps he identifies could have negative consequences? Explain your answer.

2. James B. Comey argues that police are mostly good people who sometimes fall into "mental shortcuts" that lead to racism. According to Comey, how do these mental shortcuts develop? What needs to happen, in Comey's view, to fix such shortcuts or prevent them from forming in the first place? Use information from the viewpoint to support your response.

3. Carolyn Davis believes that militarized police are unnecessary and dangerous in a society that is already so socially and racially divided, and that police militarization contributes to the rise of state aggression. Do you agree that armored police forces are inherently bad? Are they symbols of the government's attempts to oppress minorities? Can situations arise in which the police should arm themselves with such militaristic weapons? Explain your reasoning.

Chapter 2

1. Colin Ochs argues that the problem of police brutality in the United States is growing to "epidemic" proportions. Jack Kerwick claims that the police brutality epidemic is "a lie" and that most people who request police assistance

are satisfied with officers' response and would request police assistance again. Which author presents the stronger argument? Explain your answer, citing details from both viewpoints.

2. Donovan X. Ramsey believes white Americans must take responsibility for defending black Americans from police brutality. Do you think police violence is truly skewed against African Americans? Can white Americans more effectively intervene against this? Explain.

3. Joseph Kishore claims that classism contributes to police brutality in the United States more so than racism does. What evidence does Kishore provide to support his claim? Do you agree or disagree with his opinion? Explain your answer.

Chapter 3

1. Shahid Buttar writes that police body cameras would not solve the problem of police brutality because the cameras would provide insight only into particular instances, not complete behavioral patterns. Is he correct about this? Or could referring to all of the camera recordings by one police officer help investigators form a more complete picture of that officer's practices on the job? Explain your reasoning.

2. Charlie Dent argues that Americans can discuss the deficiencies of their police forces but should not protest the police, for this disrespects the people who risk their lives to protect their communities. Is Dent correct about this? Are protests against police inherently disrespectful? Or should Americans be able to exercise their freedom of speech in any manner they choose, against whomever they choose, without fear of criticism? Why, or why not?

3. Michael S. Rozeff proposes introducing volunteer civilian police forces to American law enforcement so abusive police departments will be forced to reform to compete. Do

you think this solution is realistic? Can civilian police become a legitimate law enforcement power in America, or do you think citizens will be reluctant to trust newly formed and untested police agencies in their neighborhoods? Explain.

Chapter 4

1. Barry Sussman believes the Department of Justice should prosecute members of the Ferguson Police Department for misconduct instead of simply recommending reforms. Do you agree with Sussman that reforms are not enough to correct police brutality? Must violent officers also be held accountable for their actions? Explain.

2. Paul Joseph Watson believes police brutality has nothing to do with race but rather is related to law enforcement's militarized attitude of seeing citizens as their enemies. Do you think police brutality is caused only by the attitudes of individual officers? Does racism play a role? Explain.

3. Imani Gandy writes that the Justice Department should not be expected to prosecute individual cases of police brutality, for doing so would require it to prove the intent of the officers, a nearly impossible task. Rather, the department should focus on finding and reforming long-term practices of police misconduct. Should Americans not expect the federal government to seek justice against individual officers simply because it would prove difficult? Could the Justice Department attempt to indict violent officers just as it does any other suspected criminals? Explain.

Organizations to Contact

The editors have compiled the following list of organizations concerned with the issues debated in this book. The descriptions are derived from materials provided by the organizations. All have publications or information available for interested readers. The list was compiled on the date of publication of the present volume; the information provided here may change. Be aware that many organizations take several weeks or longer to respond to inquiries, so allow as much time as possible.

American Civil Liberties Union (ACLU)
125 Broad Street, 18th Floor, New York, NY 10004
(212) 549-2500
website: www.aclu.org

Founded in 1920, the American Civil Liberties Union (ACLU) is a nonprofit organization dedicated to promoting and protecting the civil rights of all American citizens. It accomplishes this goal by litigating civil liberties issues in court while lobbying the US Congress for action on civil rights abuses in the United States. The ACLU condemns the use of excessive force by police, particularly when it targets minority groups. The organization collaborates with police departments to reduce their use of violence and ensure accountability for abusive officers. Numerous articles, press releases, and blog posts on police brutality, including "Acting and Directing with Police Cameras" and "The ACLU Response to Ferguson," can be accessed on the ACLU's website.

Amnesty International
5 Penn Plaza, 16th Floor, New York, NY 10001
(212) 807-8400 • fax: (212) 627-1451
e-mail: aimember@aiusa.org
website: www.amnestyusa.org

Amnesty International is a nongovernmental organization dedicated to ending all violations of human rights. It researches and reports on all cases of abuse around the world and subsequently petitions governments for change. In the United States, Amnesty International has worked to eradicate police brutality by calling on Congress to institute a system of reforms. Changes would include laws to stop racial profiling by police and a national commission to review and report on cases of police misconduct. Amnesty International publishes reports on international human rights abuses, including police brutality, on its website. One such report is "Good Practice for Law Enforcement Officials Policing Demonstrations."

Cato Institute
1000 Massachusetts Avenue NW
Washington, DC 20001-5403
(202) 842-0200
website: www.cato.org

The Cato Institute is a libertarian think tank founded in 1977. It espouses the principles of limited government and maximized civil liberties for all Americans. As such, the institute has denounced American police misconduct as a symptom of state aggression, which, it claims, exerts unconstitutional powers while alienating Americans from their government. The Cato Institute's main publication is the *Cato Journal*. The organization also has published a diverse range of articles and commentaries on the state of police brutality in the United States. Titles such as "Baltimore Burning: It's Not a Matter of Money. We Tried That" and "Video of Walter Scott Killing Is but a Glimpse of Police Misconduct" can be accessed online.

Communities United Against Police Brutality (CUAPB)
4200 Cedar Avenue S, Minneapolis, MN 55407
website: www.cuapb.org

Communities United Against Police Brutality (CUAPB) is a Minneapolis-based organization dedicated to ending police brutality in the United States. Along with promoting this vision, the group helps survivors of police brutality recover from their experiences and begin fighting for an end to police abuse. The CUAPB has released several documents relating to police brutality in America that can be viewed online. These include "CUAPB List of 31 Actions for Improving Minneapolis Police" and "Police-Community Relations, Body Cams and the Cooptation of the Community Agenda."

Leadership Conference on Civil and Human Rights
1629 K Street NW, 10th Floor, Washington, DC 20006
(202) 466-3311
website: www.civilrights.org

The Leadership Conference on Civil and Human Rights is composed of more than two hundred separate organizations around the country that work to increase the freedom and civil rights of all Americans. Aside from its advocacy, the conference actively lobbies American lawmakers to implement more progressive, inclusive civil rights legislation. The organization opposes police brutality and has written about its effects on American citizens in its online reports and commentaries. The conference also writes of related issues in its quarterly publication *Civil Rights Monitor*. Articles on the conference's press webpage include "Discrimination in the Criminal Justice System."

National Association for the Advancement of Colored People (NAACP)
4805 Mt. Hope Drive, Baltimore, MD 21215
(410) 580-5777
website: www.naacp.org

The National Association for the Advancement of Colored People (NAACP) was founded in 1909 as a civil rights group for African Americans. It advocates for rights and the fair and equal treatment of all African Americans. In 2014 and 2015, the NAACP spoke out against police brutality, specifically the targeting of African Americans for unlawful arrests. The NAACP supports its own online blog and publishes a variety of news articles, summaries, and reports on issues related to African Americans. News stories about police brutality such as "NAACP Focuses on Officer-Involved Shootings" can be accessed online.

National Police Accountability Project (NPAP)
499 Seventh Avenue 12N, New York, NY 10018
(212) 630-9939 • fax: (212) 659-0695
e-mail: npap@nlg.org
website: www.nlg-npap.org

The nonprofit National Police Accountability Project (NPAP) is dedicated to eradicating police brutality throughout the United States by taking legal action against such behavior. An organization of the National Lawyers Guild, NPAP consists of plaintiffs' lawyers, law students, and legal workers who seek to educate the American public on what they can do to combat police brutality. Information relating to police violence—including web links, research papers, and reports—can be found on NPAP's website. Articles include "Copwatching" and "Police Indemnification."

Reason Foundation
5737 Mesmer Avenue, Los Angeles, CA 90230
(310) 391-2245 • fax: (310) 391-4395
website: www.reason.org

The Reason Foundation is a libertarian think tank that advocates for the principles of personal freedom, free markets, and a small national government. It produces a large amount of peer-reviewed research to offer solutions to national problems. The foundation has denounced police brutality and has published a wealth of articles and opinion pieces on the issue in its magazine, *Reason*. Articles such as "Cop Fires Gun Through Rolled Up Window to Shoot and Kill Unarmed Des Moines Man" and "McKinney: Of Pool Parties, Police Brutality, and Institutional Racism" can be accessed on the publication's website, Reason.com.

Southern Poverty Law Center (SPLC)
400 Washington Avenue, Montgomery, AL 36104
(334) 956-8200
website: www.splcenter.org

The Southern Poverty Law Center (SPLC) advocates for justice for the marginalized factions of the American people by tracking and exposing American hate groups; lobbying for legislation against discrimination; and educating the public about hate, discrimination, and equality. The SPLC monitors police brutality throughout the United States and has thoroughly commented on such incidents. The organization has published news and commentary articles on police brutality on its blog, *Hatewatch*, and regularly writes of related issues in its diverse selection of reports and magazines, which are available for download online.

US Department of Justice (DOJ)

950 Pennsylvania Avenue NW, Washington, DC 20530-0001
(202) 514-2000
e-mail: press@usdoj.gov
website: www.justice.gov

The US Department of Justice (DOJ) is a division of the federal government's judicial branch, responsible for enforcing the law throughout the United States. The DOJ has spoken out against police brutality, decrying the practice as an unconstitutional violation of Americans' civil rights. It also has investigated numerous police departments around the country, rooting out abusive behavior and forcing police to reform. Prominent examples of the DOJ's findings in such investigations include the reports "Investigation of the Cleveland Division of Police" and "Investigation of the Ferguson Police Department," both of which examine police brutality and may be accessed online.

Bibliography of Books

Michelle Alexander — *The New Jim Crow: Mass Incarceration in the Age of Colorblindness*. New York: New Press, 2010.

Radley Balko — *Rise of the Warrior Cop: The Militarization of America's Police Forces*. New York: PublicAffairs, 2013.

Tony Bouza — *Expert Witness: Breaking the Policeman's Blue Code of Silence*. Brookline, MA: A Bigger Play, 2013.

Arthur Browne — *One Righteous Man: Samuel Battle and the Shattering of the Color Line in New York*. Boston: Beacon Press, 2015.

Cheryl K. Chumley — *Police State USA: How Orwell's Nightmare Is Becoming Our Reality*. Washington, DC: WND Books, 2014.

Jonathon A. Cooper — *Twentieth-Century Influences on Twenty-First Century Policing: Continued Lessons of Police Reform*. Lanham, MD: Lexington Books, 2015.

Joe Domanick — *Blue: The LAPD and the Battle to Redeem American Policing*. New York: Simon & Schuster, 2015.

Charles R. Epp, Steven Maynard-Moody, and Donald P. Haider-Markel — *Pulled Over: How Police Stops Define Race and Citizenship*. Chicago: University of Chicago Press, 2014.

Colin Flaherty — *'Don't Make the Black Kids Angry': The Hoax of Black Victimization and Those Who Enable It*. Seattle, WA: CreateSpace, 2015.

John Fund and Hans von Spakovsky — *Obama's Enforcer: Eric Holder's Justice Department*. New York: Broadside Books, 2014.

Ronnie Greene — *Shots on the Bridge: Police Violence and Cover-Up in the Wake of Katrina*. Boston: Beacon Press, 2015.

Scott Hampton — *Culturism: Why African-Americans Must Stop Blaming Racism for Their Problems and Start Taking Full Responsibility*. Lehigh Press, 2014.

Rodney King and Lawrence J. Spagnola — *The Riot Within: My Journey from Rebellion to Redemption*. New York: HarperOne, 2012.

Michael Matthews — *We Are the Cops: The Real Lives of America's Police*. New York: Silvertail Books, 2015.

Kevin B. O'Connell — *The Case for Probable Cause: A Study of the Darren Wilson/Michael Brown Grand Jury Decision*. Seattle, WA: CreateSpace, 2014.

| Paul Craig Roberts | *How America Was Lost: From 9/11 to the Police/Welfare State*. Atlanta, GA: Clarity Press, 2014. |

Wendy Ruderman and Barbara Laker — *Busted: A Tale of Corruption and Betrayal in the City of Brotherly Love.* New York: HarperCollins, 2014.

Bernard Schaffer — *Way of the Warrior: The Philosophy of Law Enforcement.* Seattle, WA: CreateSpace, 2013.

Gerry Spence — *Police State: How America's Cops Get Away with Murder.* New York: St. Martin's Press, 2015.

Anthony Stanford — *Copping Out: The Consequences of Police Corruption and Misconduct.* Santa Barbara, CA: Praeger, 2015.

Bryan Stevenson — *Just Mercy: A Story of Justice and Redemption.* New York: Spiegel & Grau, 2014.

Lori Beth Way and Ryan Patten — *Hunting for "Dirtbags": Why Cops Over-Police the Poor and Racial Minorities.* Boston: Northeastern University Press, 2013.

John W. Whitehead — *A Government of Wolves: The Emerging American Police State.* New York: SelectBooks, 2013.

Kristian Williams — *Our Enemies in Blue: Police and Power in America.* Oakland, CA: AK Press, 2015.

Sherman Williams   *Killer Cop: Unnecessary Use of Deadly Physical Force and How to Protect Yourself from Being Shot.* Seattle, WA: CreateSpace, 2015.

Khalfani B. Yabuku   *When the Thin Blue Line Begins to Blur: Memoirs of an Atlanta Police Commander's Struggle to Maintain Accountability Within the APD.* Khalfani B. Yabuku, 2015.

Index

A

ABC News survey, of police brutality, 101
ACLU. *See* American Civil Liberties Union
Afghanistan war, 58
African Americans
    stop and frisk searches, 44, 74–75
    targeting by police, 14, 108, 130, 163–164
    2014/2015 deaths, 19
Alabama state police, 14
Alcoholic Beverage Control (AB) police, 162
American Civil Liberties Union (ACLU)
    mentally disabled victims filings, 163
    militarism lawsuits, 58
    Ohio office, 82
    report on targeting blacks, 44
    smartphone application development, 16
    view of surveillance cameras, 117
Anaheim Police Department, 118
Apuzzo, Matt, 58
Arel, Dan, 56–57
Aveni, Thomas, 73

B

Balko, Radley, 63
Barr, Bob, 62
Bay State Examiner article, 89–90

Beatty, Joyce, 170
Beavercreek, Ohio, 169, 170, 171
Bedford-Stuyvesant, New York, 134–135
Bell, Sean, 80
Belmar, Jon, 64
Better Government Association, 129
Biden, Joe, 180
Bill of Rights, 19
Black Entertainment Television (BET), 105
Black Lives Matter movement, 123
Black Panther Party for Self-Defense, 130, 131
Blackwell, Jeffrey, 85
Body cameras
    cons of using, 124
    expanding police use, 117, 121
    Harrison, Jason, police shooting, 165
    helpfulness *vs.* insufficient, 127–132
    mass incarceration impact, 123
    Mesa, Arizona, study, 118
    Obama, Barack, support for, 121
    pilot programs, trial runs, 118, 180, 200–201
    potential impact, 37–38
    reduced complaints when used, 76
    stopping police brutality, strengths, 115–119
    stopping police brutality, weaknesses, 120–126

transparency promises, 122–123, 125
United Kingdom study, 118
United States studies, 31, 38, 76, 116–117, 118
See also Cell phone and video recordings
Bratton, Bill, 52–53, 79, 136
Brennan Center for Justice (NYU School of Law), 170
Brickner, Mike, 83–84
Brinsley, Ismaaiyl Abdullah, 134–135, 141
Brown, Michael, killing (Ferguson, Missouri)
    absence of indictments, 139, 180, 188
    Chemerensky, Erwin, comments, 84
    community solutions, 125
    DOJ probe and report, 32, 44, 118, 159, 160, 163–164, 166, 184, 194, 197–198
    Holder, Eric, investigation, 85, 159, 164, 166
    inappropriate police action, 63
    Occupy 2.0 reaction, 176
    O"Mara, Mark, comments, 85
    onset of national dialogue, 149
    parents statement of condemnation, 135
    police claims, 128
    Serpico, Frank, accusations, 70
    shooting death, 19, 31, 42, 43, 62, 65, 70, 78, 88, 105
    statement by family, 135
    violations of African Americans rights, 19, 20
    whites' views or police response, 108
Brown, Sherrod, 171

Buchner, Brian, 149–150, 151, 152, 153, 155
Bundy, Cliven, 134
Bush, George W., 106, 125
Buttar, Shahid, 120–126

C

Caputo, Angela, 130
Carey, Miriam, 103
Cell phone and video recordings
    confiscation by police, 16
    demands for proof, 24
    Garner, Eric, confrontation, 15, 128
    Gray, Freddie, shooting, 31
    Mobile Justice application, 16
    North Charleston confrontation, 16
    Scott, Walter, shooting, 37
    Staten Island confrontation, 15
    See also Body cameras
Center for Constitutional Rights (CCR), 80, 82
Central Intelligence Agency (CIA), 106, 122
Charney, Darius, 80, 82
Chemerensky, Erwin, 84–85
Chicago Alliance Against Racist and Political Repression, 129
Chicago Police Department (CPD)
    abuse complaints, 72, 74
    interviews with officers, 64
    lying by officers, 89
    misconduct cases, 129
    police brutality incident, 91
    reasons for becoming police, 50
    shooting of African Americans, 130

targeting African Americans, 130

Childress, Sarah, 193–201

Choke hold death. *See under* Garner, Eric

Christopher Commission (Los Angeles), 79–80

CiCi's Restaurant, 134

Cincinnati Collaborative Agreement, 82

Citizen Police Review Board (Cincinnati), 83–84

Civilian oversight
advantages, 149–152
benefits, disadvantages, 148–156
obstacles, 154–156
organization recommendation, 144, 146–147, 152–154
special police training, 145

Civilian police forces, 56

Civil Rights Division (U.S. DOJ), 41, 159

Comey, James B., 33, 35, 46–54

Community Oriented Policing Services (COPS), 96

Cooper, Brittney, 107

Cop Block, 92, 149

Crawford, John, III, 88, 103, 169, 172

Criminal Justice and Behavior study (2007), 35

Criminal Justice Policy Review study (2012), 35

Cure Violence program, 128, 130

D

Davidson, Mark, 14

Davis, Carolyn, 55–60

De Blasio, Bill, 82
antipolice campaign rhetoric, 141
comment on lack of indictments, 99
NYPD protests against, 114, 135, 141
Pataki, George, blaming of, 135
sympathy with protestors, 113–114

DeGioai, John J., 47

Democratic Party, 108, 125

Dent, Charlie, 137–141

DeWine, Mike, 171

Diallo, Amadou, 80, 82

DiAngelo, Robin, 101–102

DOJ. *See* U.S. Department of Justice

Domanick, Joe, 79, 85–86

E

End Racial Profiling Act (ERPA), 125, 126

Eyre, Pete, 148–156

F

Facebook, 88, 92, 102

Fairfield, Ohio, 169

FBI (Federal Bureau of Investigations), 131
Ferguson, Missouri, investigation, 159
limited grasp of problem, 33–34
racial profiling comment, 35, 37
statistics on homicides, 176

study of King, Martin Luther, Jr., 48–49
view of police handling of incidents, 33
Federal government
  combating police brutality, 168–172
  failures correcting police brutality, 161–167
  handing out weapons, 79
  investigation of Ferguson, 20
  lowering expectations for, 187, 191
  police abuse report, 143
  post-Sept. 11 funding, 64
  settlement with Cleveland police, 190
Ferguson, Missouri (Michael Brown incident)
  ABC News survey, 101
  absence of indictments, 139, 180, 188
  Beavercreek, Ohio, comparison, 170
  body camera program, 118
  citizen-police confrontation, 48, 56–57
  civil rights violations by police, 160
  community demands, 125
  community-police disconnect, 48
  declaration of emergency, 105
  divided views of whites, 108
  DOJ investigation findings, 44, 163–164
  DOJ recommendations, 198, 200
  government confirmation of violations, 20
  government's limited actions, 163

grand jury absence of indictments, 31
grassroots activism, 121, 180
Holder, Eric, involvement, 166
inappropriate police action, 63
limited legal accountability, 84
NACOLE engagement with, 149
Occupy 2.0 reaction, 176
police militarization, 56–57, 59–60, 62–64, 66
police reforms, 191
post-incident reforms, 83–85, 191, 198, 200
protests and riots, 31, 33, 43, 47, 53, 62, 85, 116, 139, 175
racial divisions, 32
Serpico, Frank, accusations, 70
targeting African Americans, 19, 20, 32
See also Brown, Michael, killing
First Coast News (Georgia), 92
FiveThirtyEight, journalism outlet, 34–35
Flatow, Nicole, 77–86
Ford, Ezell, 80, 103
Fourth Amendment (Constitution), 19–20
Fraternal Order of Police (FOP), 41, 102
The FreeThoughtProject.com, 92
Fund, John, 62

G

Garner, Eric
  ABC News comment, 101
  begging with police, 176

choke hold death, 31, 42, 47, 88, 95, 105, 113, 135, 179, 189, 194–195
de Blasio, Bill, comment, 99
grand jury lack of indictment, 139, 179, 180, 188, 189
homicide ruling, 128
last words, 113
makeshift memorial for, 136
Obama, Barack, comment, 106, 174, 185–186
police evasion of justice, 121
protests against death, 47
socioeconomic class, 107–108
video of confrontation, 15, 42, 99, 122, 139
white supremacy interpretation, 106–107
YouTube video of incident, 122
Gates, Daryl, 79
Giuliani, Rudy, 135
Goodson, Caesar, 31
Gray, Freddie, 31
Great Britain, 19–20
Great Depression (1930s), 109

H

Harrison, Jason, 162–163, 165
Harris polls, on white Americans, racism, 100
Hoffmeister, Thaddeus, 171
Holder, Eric
    anti-police brutality meeting, 180
    body cameras funding, 118
    civil rights violations investigations, 169

Ferguson, Missouri, investigation, 20, 85, 159, 160, 164, 188, 194
    hesitance to prosecute, 166
    launching of initiatives, 181
    Pataki, George, blaming of, 135
    probing police misconduct, 168–172
    See also U.S. Department of Justice
Hoover, J. Edgar, 49, 131

I

Indiana, self-defense law (2012), 130
Institutional racism, 42
International Socialist Organization (ISO), 107
Investor's Business Daily editorial, 62
Iraq war, 58, 59

J

John Jay College of Criminal Justice, 79, 7979
Johnson, Hank, 63
Johnson, Lyndon, 40, 41
    panel examining police practices, 40–41, 43
Johnson, Martese, 162
Jordan, Jim, 171

K

Kasich, John, 171
Kennedy, Robert, 49
Kerner Commission report (1968), 40–41, 43, 45

Kerwick, Jack, 93–97

Killed by Police database (Facebook), 88, 92

King, Martin Luther, Jr.
FBI interaction, 48
Hoover, J. Edgar, wiretap request, 49
1968 assassination, 41

King, Rodney, 14–15
beating by police, 14, 43, 99, 179, 195
bystander video of incident, 78–80, 99
impact of publicity, 37
post-verdict riots, 65, 81
prosecution of officers, 189, 191

Kishore, Joseph, 104–110

Kovac, Matthew, 127–132

Kristian, Bonnie, 71–76

Ku Klux Klan, 113

L

Las Vega, Nevada, 134

Law enforcement
application of federal laws, 166
civilian oversight, benefits, disadvantages, 148–156
civilian police forces, 56
Comey, James B., opinion, 46–54
community policing strategies, 32–33
current issues, 48
cynical attitudes, 50
DOJ intervention, 159
DOJ investigations, 196
DOJ legislation, 189–190, 195
DOJ monitoring failures, 143

FBI justifiable homicide data, 34–35
mishandling mentally ill persons, 149, 162–163, 165
monitoring by oversight boards, 149–153
mourning police officer deaths, 29
NY/LA, city-level approval, 100–101
Obama, Barack, recommendations, 40
post-L.A. riots reforms, 31
public view of, 139, 162
racial profiling, 35
racism and violence, 57, 58, 179–180
radical reorganization suggestion, 144–147
recommendation for valuing, 137–141
relationship with communities, 40, 42, 47, 53
role of, 28
role of justice, 101
UN questions about U.S., 184
vigilantism, 146
See also Body cameras; Police militarization; Police officers

License plate information, 25–26

Liu, Wenjian, 47, 138, 141

Livingston, Chris, 165

Los Angeles Police Department (LAPD)
acquittal of police officers, 14, 43, 81
body camera pilot program, 118
consent decree imposition, 190
King incident-related riots, 31, 43

militaristic actions, 78–79
Rampart Division scandal, 190
U.S. DOJ investigation, 194
See also King, Rodney
Lynch, Patrick, 114, 128, 135
Lynn, Massachusetts police department, 89–90

M

Madison, James, 19
Manassas Junction Police Department, 145
Manning, Darrin, 72
Mapping Police Violence, research collaborative, 91
Marshall, Josh, 56–57
Martin, Trayvon, 100, 169
Mass incarceration
body cameras, impact, 121, 123, 126
Obama, Barack, initiatives, 181
refusals in addressing, 186
McLay, Cameron, 102
McQuillan, Howard, 102
Meanes, Pamela J., 149, 150, 153
Mentally ill persons
Harrison, Jason, police shooting death, 162–163, 165
San Francisco shooting, 163
Thomas, Kelly, death, 149
training for dealing with, 83, 196
Middle East wars, 58
Militarization. *See* Police militarization
Miller, Amanda and Jerad, 134
Minnesota, police violence, 73
Mobile Justice smartphone app, 16

Morrison, Grant, 88, 89
My Brother's Keeper initiative, 51

N

National Advisory Commission on Civil Disorders, 41
National Association for Civilian Oversight of Law Enforcement (NACOLE), 149
National Bar Association, 149
National Guard, 105
Nation journal, 108
New Jersey, police brutality, corruption, 74
Newton, Huey P., 131
New York City
approval of police, 100–101
Bratton, Bill, police tactics, 79
brutality investigations, 122–123
citizen lawsuits against police, 78, 82
citizen-police disconnect, 48, 52–53
Davidson, Mark, arrest, 14
Diallo, Amadou, brutality incident, 80–82
Garner, Eric, arrest, death, 15, 42, 47
protests and riots, 15–16, 113
New York City Police Department (NYPD)
anti-de Blasio protest, 114, 135, 141
Bratton, Bill, comments, 52–53
failure of police indictments, 99, 139
forced reforms, 191

Garner case evasions of justice, 121
murder of police officers, 47–48, 94, 136, 138
oversight committee, 82
Patrolmen's Benevolent Association, 128
stock and frisk overuse, 80, 122–123
See also Serpico, Frank
New York Civil Liberties Union, 80
New York Times article, 99
North Charleston, South Carolina, 16
Nutter, Michael, 44
NYU School of Law, 170

O

Obama, Barack
anti-police brutality meeting, 180
BET interview, 105–106
body cameras initiative, 121
corruption accusations against, 109
Giuliani, Rudy, blaming of, 135
launching of initiatives, 181
My Brother's Keeper initiative, 51
panel recommendations, 44
police practices panel, 40, 43
separation of brutality from racism, cons, 178–185
separation of brutality from racism, pros, 173–177
Sharpton, Al, appeal to, 106
speeches on race, 99–100, 105–106

support for body cameras, 121
supposed transformative candidacy of, 108–109
Task Force on 21st Century Policing, 200–201
willingness to speak out, 51
Obama, Michelle, 106
Occupy movement, 149, 176
Ochs, Colin, 87–92
Office of Community Oriented Policing Services (DOJ), 96
Ohio, stop and frisk violence, 72
O'Mara, Mark, 85
Orta, Ramsey, 15
Orwell, George, 162

P

Pantaleo, Daniel, 15–16, 174, 179, 188–189, 191
See also Garner, Eric
Parker, Neykeyia, 72
Pataki, George, 135
Patheos.com, 56–57
Patrolmen's Benevolent Association (PBA), 128
Pattern or practice report (DOJ), 32, 172, 188–190, 196, 197, 198–199
Peduto, Bill, 102
Pew Research Center survey (2014), 32
Philadelphia Police Department (PDD), 44
Pieklo, Jessica Mason, 188
Pittsburgh Police Department, 102
Police brutality
ABC News survey, 101

body cameras, helpfulness,
127–132
citizen oversight solution,
142–147
class *vs.* race orientation, 104–
110
community solutions, 130,
132
conflicting information on,
30–38
Diallo, Amadou, incident,
80–82
epidemic U.S. growth, no,
93–97
epidemic U.S. growth, yes,
87–92
government prevention, failures, 161–167
government prevention suc-
cesses, 168–172
Harris polls, 100
improvement variability,
77–76
ineffectiveness of body cameras, 120–126
need for citizen protests, 133–
136
need for stopping, 21–29
New Jersey, 74
Obama, Barack, comment,
106
racism as non separate, 178–
186
racism as separate, 173–177
racism *vs.* minorities, 39–45
role of civilian oversight, 142–
147
systemic *vs.* anecdotal, 71–76
U.S. DOJ helpfulness, no,
187–192
U.S. DOJ helpfulness, yes,
193–201

U.S. protests against, 133–136
varied results at improving,
77–86
white American's silence as
consent, 98–103
See also specific incidents
Police Executive Research Forum,
64
Police militarization
Ferguson, Missouri, 56–57,
62–64, 66, 85
Los Angeles Police Department, 79
public safety needs, 61–66
racist systems, 59
United States problems, 55–60
use of weaponry, 58
weaponry, tactics, 57, 58
worsening of, 78, 177
*Police Officer Body-Worn Cameras:
Assessing the Evidence* report
(DOJ), 38
Police officers
Brinsley, Ismaaiyl, murder of,
134–135, 141
citizen trust factors, 23–24
false resisting arrest claims,
164
Garner, Eric, choke hold
death, 31, 42, 88
harassment/profiling behavior,
26
license plate information requests, 22
mishandling mentally ill persons, 149, 162–163, 165
primary role, 27–28
racism against minorities, no,
46–54
racism against minorities, yes,
39–45

trained observer status, 22–23, 24

video recordings of, 16

See also Law enforcement

Police Policy Studies Council, 73

Police-Public Contact Survey (PPCS), 96

ProPublica report (2014), 35

R

Racial bias, 49–50, 184

Racial profiling
degree and severity, 26
existence in law enforcement, 35
national database tracking, 28
need for ending, 125, 181, 195
NYC Police Department, 72
unconstitutionality of, 82

Ramirez, Richard, 88, 89

Ramos, Rafael, 47, 138, 141

Rampart Division scandal (LAPD), 190

Ramsey, Charles, 44

Ramsey, Donovan X., 98–103

Reno News and Review series, 149–156

Republican Party, 125

Resisting arrest
Brown, Michael, 138
false claims by officers, 164
media/police blotter practice, 130
prerequisite conviction for, 24–25

Reynoso, Denis, 89

RH Reality Check, 188

Rialto, California, 31, 38, 76, 116–117

Rice, Tamir, 31, 88, 99, 136, 190, 195

Rikers Island prison complex, 15

Rise of the Warrior Cop (Balko), 75

Roberson, Jack Lamar, 92

Rolling Stone article, 107

Rothman, Noah, 62

Rowe, Richard, 21–29

Rozeff, Michael S., 142–147

Russell, Katheryn K., 74

S

Safir, Howard, 80

Salon.com, 107

Santana, Feidin, 16

Schiff, Adam, 115–119

Scott, Walter
Slager, Michael, shooting, 16, 31, 99, 100, 103
smartphone recording of shooting, 37
Supreme Court decision, 34

Scott v. Harris (2007), 34

Selma, Alabama, 14

Serpico, Frank, 69–70

Sharpton, Al, 106

Shaw, Jazz, 61–66

Silence, of white Americans, as consent, 98–103

Slager, Michael T., 16, 31

Smartphone recordings. *See* Cell phone and video recordings

Social inequality, in the U.S., 108–109

South Asian wars, 58

Southwest Journal of Criminal Justice paper (2010), 37

Special duties amendment, 26–28

Spinney, Jessica, 89

Stanford University study (2014), 38

Stanley-Jones, Aiyana, 103

Stewart, Carter M., 169

St. Louis County Police Department, 64

Stop and frisk campaign
  brutality incidents, 72
  Florida, 74–75
  increasing incidents, 82
  New York City violence, 72–73, 80
  targeting African Americans, 44

Sullivan, Ronald, 170

Sussman, Barry, 161–167

SWAT teams, 58, 65, 75

Systemic police brutality, 71–76

T

Talking Points Memo, 56–57

Task Force on 21st Century Policing, 43, 200–201

Taylor, Jonathan S., 149, 150, 151–152, 154–155

Taylor, Keeanga-Yamahtta, 107, 178–186

Tea Party, 134

Terrill, William, 73

Thomas, Kelly, 149

Thomas, Timothy, 82–84

Thompson, Juan, 133–136

Trained observer status (of police officers), 22–23, 24

Twitter, 102, 135, 174

U

UN Human Rights Council, 14

U.S. Bureau of Justice, 96

U.S. Congress
  civilian oversight opposition, 41
  creation of DOJ, 160
  problem ignored by, 121–122
  resource creation, 118–119
  Sharpton, Al, appeal to, 106

U.S. Department of Justice (DOJ)
  agreements with advocacy groups, 83
  body camera funding, study, 118–119
  Brown, Michael, report, 32, 44, 118, 159, 160, 163–164, 166, 184, 194, 197–198
  Civil Rights Division, 41, 159
  Community Oriented Policing Services, 96
  creation of by Congress, 160
  investigation of LAPD, 194, 197
  investigations of police departments, 20, 159, 160, 163–164, 184
  limits in correcting police brutality, 187–192
  monitoring failures, 143
  Office of Community Oriented Policing Services, 96
  pattern or practice report, 32, 172, 188–190, 196, 197, 198–199
  Police Officer Body-Worn Cameras report, 38
  report of police officers' report, 75
  resources for local governments, 118–119

role in correcting police brutality, 193–201
study of police self-reporting,
75
See also Holder, Eric
U.S. House of Representatives, 62
U.S. Office of the Attorney General, 159
U.S. Supreme Court, 159

V

Video recordings. *See* Cell phone
and video recordings
Violent Crime Control and Law
Enforcement Act (1994), 159,
189

W

Wall Street, financial crash, 106
Wall Street Journal article (2012),
95
Washington, Linn, Jr., 39–45
Washington Post article, 63
Watson, Paul Joseph, 173–177

What Does It Mean to Be White?
(DiAngelo), 101–102
White, Michael D., 38
White American's silence as con-
sent, 98–103
Wihbey, John, 30–38
Wilson, Darren
Brown, Michael, killing, 19,
31, 42, 62, 70, 138–139, 179
DOJ investigation of shooting,
188–189, 194
minimal prosecution likeli-
hood, 191
See also Brown, Michael

X

X, Malcolm, 131

Y

Youlen, Michael, 145
YouTube videos, 16–17, 122

Z

Zimmerman, George, 100, 169